PYTHON PROGRAMMING Crash Course

A Crash Course Guide to Learn Programming Python, all you Need to Learn for Introducing you in the Programming World.

By

Robert Campbell

Book One

PYTHON PROGRAMMING FOR BEGINNERS

The Complete Guide for Total Beginner to Learn Python Programming in 1 week.

Introduction

Programming is becoming an increasingly demanded skill for anything from web design to Machine Learning and the Internet of Things.

It's on its way to having a daily use due to the importance of technology.

While programming used to be a subject that people started studying for their computer science degree, now it is often taught starting from elementary school.

One of the main reasons for its widespread use is accessibility.

You don't need much to get started.

Thanks to the power of the Internet, all you need is a computer and a number of software tools that you can download and install without spending a penny.

In addition, there are many resources to learn from, as well as organized communities you can join and learn from.

You are going to learn why Python is one of the best programming languages to start with, as well as progress your career if this isn't your first language.

Furthermore, you will explore the tools you need, install them, and start your journey.

This will guide you step by step and show you everything you need to know in order to get started.

If you are already familiar with any other programming language such as C, C++, or Java, you might want to skip this or simply glance through it to refresh your memory.

We can define programming as the process of designing, coding, debugging, and maintaining the source code of a computer program, which means that we say the steps to follow for the creation of the source code of computer programs.

The programming language, are all those rules or regulations, symbols, and particular words used for the creation of a program, and with it, offer a solution to a particular problem.

The best-known programming languages are: Basic (1964), C++ (1983), Python (1991), Java (1995), C# (2000), among others.

Programming is one of the stages for software development; programming specifies the structure and behavior of a program, verifying if it is working properly or not.

Programming includes the specification of the algorithm defined as the sequence of steps and operations that the program must perform to solve a problem, for the algorithm to work, the program must be implemented in a compatible and correct language.

We could consider programming even easier than learning a new language because the programming language will be governed by a set of rules, which are, generally, always similar, so you could say that it might be considered as a natural language.

In order to better understand the subject of programming, we could start with the beginnings of programming and how all this universe of languages and programs we know today began.

We could start saying that programming began when the first computer was created in the fifteenth century, when a machine capable of doing basic operations and square roots appeared (Gottfried Wilhelm von Leibniz), although the one that actually served as a great influence for the creation of the first computer was the differential machine for calculating polynomials with the support of Lady Ada Countess (1815-1852), known as the first person who entered programming, and from whom comes the name of the programming language ADA, created by the DoD (Department of the United States), in the 1970s.

Python - The First Impressions

What Is Python and Why Is It a Good Programming Language to Learn?

As a beginner who has never done anything with coding, Python is one of the best coding languages to work. Python has long been considered a beginner's language because it is so easy to learn, and you will be able to understand it right from the beginning. This is just one of the many reasons why you should choose to work with Python. You will also like there is a large active community devoted to this programming language and what's good is that it's open source so you can get started without literally having to pay anything. This language will also work on any operating system, so it won't matter which computer you want to use the language on.

Despite being the coding language that beginners like to work with, this doesn't mean that there aren't a lot of advantages that come with working with this language. Python on its own is capable of writing great codes in the process, and you can also combine it with a few other languages so that you can create as many strings of code that you like. Now, let's take some time to look at Python and all the things that you need to know to get started on using this coding language.

Why should I learn Python?

As we mentioned before, there are a lot of different coding languages that you can learn about and use. So, if there are a lot of choices out there, why would you want to go with the Python coding language in the first place? Many people, both experts, and beginners all choose to go with Python because it is easy to learn, easy to read, and it is capable of creating large, challenging codes that you might want to write. There are a lot of different reasons that you would want to work with this coding language, and these include:

- Simple enough to read

You will find that Python is a programming language that is very easy to read, even if you are a beginner. When it is compared to some of the other coding languages, it is one of the most readable languages. Since this is a natural coding language to go with, many beginners like that they can catch on so quickly and that they will understand what they are doing in no time.

- Free

Another benefit of going with Python is that it is free to use. There are some computer coding languages that you would have to pay for so you can use them and this can be quite expensive, especially if you want to learn how to use more than one of them. Python is free to use, so you don't have to worry about this problem.

- Fast

Even though this language is natural enough for any beginner to learn, Python is still considered one of the high-level languages that you can learn. This means that when you make a program and generate your codes by using Python, you will see that the execution is friendly and quick. Some coding languages are harder to work with or can't go as fast as you want them to, but this is a problem you won't have when using Python.

- Works on a variety of platforms

You can work with the Python language no matter which platform you would like to use it on. Linux is the operating system that a lot of people will choose to go with, but you can still work with Python even if you are on a Windows or Mac computer. This is excellent news because it means that you can use Python without having to make any significant changes to your current setup.

- A big library to work with

Once you start to get familiar with Python, you will notice that it comes with an extensive library. This is good news for beginners because the library is what contains all the functions, codes and other things that you need to make the language work for you. This library will help make sure that you can do some useful stuff when trying to make your code.

- A large community

Whether you have worked with coding language in the past or not, it is nice to know that there is a large community of Python users that will help you out if you ever get stuck. Any time that you need some ideas like a new project or if you have a question, or if you want to learn something new, there is a library of information to provide you with the information that you need to help you get started.

How Python Works

You know a handful of terms related to python, so let's take a step back for a second and talk about what makes python the way it is. It is an "object-oriented" programming language. To understand this, you should first know what functions are. Also known as subroutines or procedures, functions manipulate data and allow you to use code multiple times in a program without copying the code over and over again. Functions are front-and-centre when using a procedureoriented style of programming, but it doesn't always work very well when you're writing more extensive programs. That's when objectoriented programming becomes more useful. Python does not prioritize functions, but it still uses them.

Objects and classes When you combine data and function, you get an object. The Python Programiz website describes objects as a collection of data (variables) and function. In the real world, a car or house is an object. Just like every object needs a design or blueprint, every object in Python needs a class, and like design plans, classes contain all the information and details needed to create the object. That process of creation is called instantiation (which begins whenever you type in the keyword class) while the resulting object is known as an instance of a class. You use classes when you need to keep data related to each other organized and grouped.

Attributes and methods

Classes need functionality attached to them, or what's the point? You achieve functionality by setting attributes, which hold the data related to functions, which in Python are known as methods. Confused? Let's look at the example HackerEarth uses:

```
class Snake:
```

```
name: "diamondhead"
```

You just created a new class, Snake, and assigned the word "name" to the word "diamondhead." That makes sense visually. Whenever you want to refer back to this information, you want the program to know that the snake name is diamondhead. The class needs to be assigned to a variable, like so:

```
snake = Snake()
```

Now, you can retrieve the attribute, which in this case is diamondhead. We should first explain the dot notation, which is a literal dot or period. Using this tells Python to look inside the space that is before the dot. Whatever is inside the space is the code that Python should execute.

You would type in:

```
print(snake.name)
```

You just told Python to look at Snake, which leads it back to Snake (), which leads it back to the class you created. When you run this program, you end up with:

```
print(snake.name)
```

diamondhead That's the essence of classes and methods. Methods are always associated with a class.

Inheritance Before moving on from classes, let's explore what inheritance means. This is the processing of reusing code, which is one of the benefits of object-oriented programming. Let's say you're continuing work on your snake project, and you want to organize the reptile into two types: water snakes and land snakes. You know that they share some characteristics, such as being legless and having flicky tongues, but there are also specific characteristics associated with the different snakes. Now, you could create two separate classes, but adding a new common characteristic would mean you have to add it into both of them, and that can quickly become annoying.

What you want to do instead is use the inheritance mechanism. You are creating a type and subtype connection between your classes. Create one class that both water and land snakes can pull - or inherit from. Your water and land snakes become sub-types, so when you add your standard features (legless, flicky tongues) to just that parent class, they show up in both sub-types. You are free to add unique and separate features into the sub-types.

Inheritance makes it way easier to keep things organized and to reuse code. You have this base or parent class that sets everything up, and if you need to modify just a piece of it or use its essential functions with some changes, you can refer back to it while creating a new subtype, and then add (to the sub-type) without messing up the parent class.

Loops Using loops can also help reduce the amount of code you have to write out every time you want the program to achieve something. Looping is not exclusive to Python; it can be employed in just about every computer language. A loop is a sequence of instructions that keep repeating within the perimeters you set up until the condition you establish is met. It allows you to execute statements or entire groups of comments multiple times without writing out the code each time.

There are two main types of loops in Python: for loops and while loops. For loops run a predetermined number of times, no matter what..

While loops will repeat a single statement or group while the given condition is correct, there is no predetermined number of times for this loop; it's all about true or false. Before beginning the loop, Python tests the condition to confirm whether or not it is true. It will keep executing a block while the state is true, and it will stop if it becomes false.

It is even possible to "nest" a loop, so you're getting a loop within the loop, or an inner loop and an outer loop. Python will cycle through the outer loop, and when it's made a full pass, it triggers the inner loop, which in turn triggers the outer loop again once its run is complete.

You can stop any type of loop by writing break and even skip over a part of code and then begin the loop again by writing continue. Why would you do this? It's advantageous if there are only certain parts of a code you want to use again. Without the option of breaking and continuing the loop, you would have to copy the entire code and then delete the part(s) you didn't want. It's much cleaner to loop. You would usually put your break and continue statement after a certain condition is met. How do you tell Python to be aware of that? You use a conditional if statement.

Conditional statements Pretty much all programming languages make use of an if statement, which is the main type of conditional statement. It is an essential part of Python's ability to make decisions about running code or not, and if necessary, change a program's flow. The if the statement is similar to a while loop in that it only runs if certain conditions are met, but unlike a while loop, conditionals only run once. Loops make use of conditional statements, but conditional statements do not require loops.

So, you tell Python you want a bit of code only if something is true. To test that, Python uses a Boolean expression, which is just a fancy way of describing a statement that is either true or false. If the answer ends up being false - the conditions are not met - what then? You will use else or elif statements. An else statement just tells the computer what the next step should be, like what block of code it should skip to instead of running the original which doesn't meet the conditions you want.

Getting ready for Python

You can run and code Python on Windows, Mac, and Linux. To get started, head over to the official website: www.python.org and download the Python installer. This book will use Windows as the primary environment for the examples and lessons.

Python 2.x vs. Python 3.x

There are two popular and official versions of Python: Python 3.x and 2.x. As of this writing, you can download Python 3.7.0 if you want the 3.x version. You can also download Python 2.7.15 if you want the 2.x version.

However, to prevent any conflicts and misunderstandings, please download and use Python 3.x. All the examples and lessons in this book are written with Python 3.x in mind.

The 2.x version is an older version of Python. Ever since the Python developers proceeded in developing Python 3.x, they have made a lot of changes to the behavior and even the syntax of the Python programming languages.

For example, if you divide 3 and 2 using the '/' operator in Python 2.x, you will receive an output of 1. If you divide the same numbers with the same operator in Python 3.x, you will receive an output of 1.5.

You may ask: If Python 3.x is new and improved, why are the developers keeping the old versions and why is Python 2.x being used?

The quick answer to that is code migration. Because there are many differences between version 2.x and version 3.x, programs and scripts created using version 2.x need to be recoded to become compatible with version 3.x Python.

If you are dealing with a small program using version 2.x, then the code migration will be a trivial problem at best. However, if you have programs with thousands of lines, then migration can become a huge problem. Other issues with migrating to Python 3.x are code maintenance and retraining programmers to adapt with the changes.

Because of the aforementioned reasons, developers with huge programs written and ran using the version 2.x runtime environment did not bother making the transition to version 3.x.

Installing the Interpreter

Python comes with two important 'programs': Python's runtime environment and command line interpreter. The Python installer you download from its website contains both. Installing them is easy, particularly in Windows.

All you need to do is download the file and click open to let it run the setup. You will need to follow a few simple step-by-step instructions, click a few buttons here and there and Python will be available on your computer.

Note that there will be a point during the installation that you will need to select the packages and features that you want to be installed in your system. Make sure that you check all of them.

Note that tcl/tk installs TkInter, which is a Graphic User Interface (GUI) toolkit you need if you plan to create windows for your programs. The

Integrated Development and Learning Environment (IDLE) require and depend on TkInter since it is a Python program with a GUI.

Also, for now, check the Python test suite feature. You will need it later. Finally, PIP is an optional feature that allows you to download Python packages later.

If you believe you do not need some of them, just make sure that the checkbox for IDLE and Python Test Suite are selected.

Using Python Shell and IDLE

There are two ways to run a Python program. And that is using its runtime environment or using the command line interpreter. The command line interpreter has two forms. The first one is the regular Python shell. The second one is IDLE or Integrated Development and Learning Environment.

The regular Python shell uses the familiar command line interface (CLI) or terminal look while IDLE is a Python program encased in a regular graphical user interface (GUI) window. IDLE is full of easy to access menu, customization options, and GUI functions while the Python shell is devoid of those and only offer a command prompt (i.e. the input field in a text-based user interface screen).

One of the beneficial functions of IDLE is its syntax highlighting. The syntax highlighting function makes it easier for programmers or scripters to identify between keywords, operators, variables, and numeric literals.

Also, you can customize the highlight color and the font properties displayed on IDLE. With the shell, you only get a monospaced font, white font color, and black background.

All of the examples in this book are written in the Python shell. However, it is okay for you to write using IDLE. It is suited for beginners since they do not need to worry about indentation and code management. Not to mention that the syntax highlighting is truly beneficial.

Writing Your First Program

To get you started, code the below Hello World program. It has been a tradition for new programmers to start their learning with this simple program. Just write this line in the shell or IDLE and press Enter.

```
>>> print("Hello World!")
Hello World!
>>> _
```

Shell, IDLE, and Scripts Syntax

Programming languages, just like a regular human language like English, have grammar/writing rules or syntax. Syntax rules in programming languages are simple but strict.

Unlike humans, the computer and computer programs like compilers and interpreters cannot understand context. They require precise and proper statements to know what you want. A simple syntax error can stop your program from functioning or make the computer put a stop on your program.

Prompt

The Python Shell and IDLE has a prompt, which looks like this: >>>. You generally start writing your code after the prompt in the Python Shell and IDLE. However, remember that when you write code in a file, py script, or module, you do not need to write the prompt.

For example:

```
Class thisClass():
    def function1():
        x = 1
        print(x)

    def function2():
        pass
```

That is valid code.

Indentation

When programming, you will encounter or create code blocks. A code block is a piece of Python program text (or statement) that can be executed as a unit, such as a module, a class definition or a function body. They often end with a colon (:).

By default and by practice, indentation is done with four spaces. You can do away with any number of spaces as long as the code block has a uniform number of spaces before each statement. For example:

```
def function1():
    x = 1
    print(x)

def function2():
            y = "Sample Text"
            print("Nothing to see here.")
```

That is perfectly valid code. You can also use tab, but it is not recommended since it can be confusing and you will get an error if you mix using tabs and spaces. Also, if you change the number of spaces for every line of code, you will get an error. Here is an example in the shell. Note the large space before print(x) on line 2.

```
>>> x = 1
```

```
>>>      print(x)
  File "<stdin>", line 1
    print(x)
    ^
IndentationError: unexpected indent
>>> _
```

By the way, a statement is a line of code or instruction.

Indentation Prompt

When using the Python Shell, it will tell you when to indent by using the prompt (...). For example:

```
>>> def function1():

        x = 1

        print(x)


>>> def function2():

        y = "Sample Text"

        print("Nothing to see here.")


>>> _
```

In IDLE, indentation will be automatic. And to escape an indentation or code block, you can just press Enter or go to the next line.

Python Shell Navigation

You cannot interact using a mouse with the Python Shell. Your mouse will be limited to the window's context menu, window commands such as minimize, maximize, and close, and scrolling.

Also, you can perform marking (selecting), copying, and pasting, but you need to use the windows context menu for that using the mouse. You can also change the appearance of the window and shell by going through the properties menu.

Most of the navigation you can do in the shell is moving the navigation caret (the blinking white underscore). You can move it using the navigation keys (left and right arrow keys, PgUp, PgDn, Home, End, etcetera). The up and down arrow keys' function is to browse through the previous lines you have written.

IDLE Navigation

The IDLE window is just like a regular GUI window. It contains a menu bar where you can access most of IDLE's functionalities. Also, you can use the mouse directly on IDLE's work area as if you are using a regular word processor.

You might need to take a quick look at the menu bar's function for you to familiarize yourself with them. Unlike the Python shell, IDLE provides a lot more helpful features that can help you with programming.

Primarily, IDLE is the main tool you can use to develop Python programs. However, you are not limited to it. You can use other development environment or word processors to create your scripts.

Troubleshooting Installation Issues

First of all, make sure that you download the installation file from the website: https://www.python.org. Next, make sure that you chose the proper installation file for your operating system. There are dedicated installation files for Windows, MacOSX, and other UNIX based operating system.

If your computer is running on Windows XP, the latest release of Python will not work on it. You must install and use Python 3.4. Also, remember that there are two versions of each release: a 32-bit and a 64-bit version. If you are unsure if your computer is running on 32 or 64-bit, then just get the 32-bit version. Normally, the recommended installer that the site will provide contains both and will automatically detect which installer it will use.

Normally, you do not need to go to Python's website to download the installation file if you are using a Linux distribution as an operating system. You can just use your system's package manager.

Before installing Python, make sure that you have at least 100 MB free disk space. You can also edit the installation location of Python. However, take note of the location you type it if you wish to install Python in a different folder.

If the installer did not provide shortcuts for you, you can just create them. The Python shell is located in the root folder of your Python installation.

<Python installation folder>\python.exe

For example:

"C:\Python37\python.exe"

For IDLE, you can use its batch file located in

<Python installation folder>\Lib\idlelib\idle.bat

For example:

"C:\Python37\Lib\idlelib\idle.bat"

If you cannot find the idlelib folder inside the Python Lib folder, reinstall Python and make sure that IDLE is checked.

The world of Variables and Operators

Variables of Python

Variable is another name for Python identifiers. Variable is a term that is used to imply a memory zone of a machine or device. In Python, you don't need to decide these kinds of factors as Python is a kind of infers programming language and is astute enough to get its variables sort.

Moreover, we may say that the Variables in Python are memory locations, having different data types, such as integers or characters. Variables in Python are just changeable and manipulable because they use a set of various operations.

In any case, variables need a letter or an underscore to get initialized. It is suggested to use lower-case letters as the variable names. In Python, sledge, and Mallet, both are two exceptional elements.

- The naming of Variables or Identifier

Factors are the situations of identifiers. A variable is used to conceive the literal coefficients and the integers used in your program. For Python, the standards to name a variable are given below.

- The essential character of an identifier must be a letter altogether, or an underscore "_".

- Each one of the characters besides the essential characters may be a letter arranged by lower case "a-z," capitals "A-Z," underscores or digits "0-9".
- A variable's name must not contain any void or empty zone, or any special or extraordinary character, such as, "! @, #, %, ^, and, *".
- A variable's name must not resemble any catchphrase portrayed in your Python program's syntax.
- In Python, variables are case sensitive. For example, i'm cool, and I'm cool isn't proportionate.
- Instances of considerable identifiers: n696, _v, v_69, etc.
- Instances of invalid identifiers: 5a, v%69, x69, etc.
- Multiple Assignments

Python enables one to maintain an incentive to various identifiers in an only explanation, which is usually called various assignments. It can be applied in two different ways either by declaring out a solitary incentive for multiple identifiers at the same time or relegating various qualities to numerous variables at different times.

Example - 1:

Open the Python console or IDE and write the command to declare variables.

```
>>> n=v=w=69

>>> print

>>> print (n, v, w)
```

Output:

When you type the command to print the value of variables, the output will be something like this.

```
>>> 69, 69, 69

>>>
```

Example – 2:

```
>>> n, v, w = 69, 74, 36

>>> print

>>> print (n)

>>> print (v)

>>> print (w)
```

Output:

For output,

When you will type your command

```
>>> print (n)
```

Your console will print "69"

When you will type your command

```
>>> print (v)
```

Your console will print "74"

When you will type your command

```
>>> print (w)
```

Your console will print "36"

Operators in Python

In general, operators are the language-specific syntactic tokens that require some action to be performed. Operators are mainly derived from the concepts of Mathematics. For example, "Sign of Multiplication (*)" is an operator used in Python programming. It is used to multiply two numbers.

In Python, operators are portrayed as a symbolic representation of a function that does a particular act between two operands to achieve some specific and desired results. Operators are viewed as the mainstays of a program on which your program works in an individual computer programming language. The assortment of operators given by Python is portrayed as pursues. Here are some commonly used operators to perform specific operations:

- Arithmetic Operators
- Comparison Operators
- Assignment Operators
- Logical Operators
- Bitwise Operators
- Membership Operators
- Identity Operators

We are going to discuss some of the above mentioned operators in this part.

- Arithmetic Operators

Arithmetic operators are used to perform particular arithmetic operations to get the desired results. In this case, two operands are taken, and between them, activity through an operator is performed, resulting in some desired, specific, and absolute value.

Here are some of the critical and useful arithmetic operators, which are commonly used in Python.

- Addition "+"
- Subtraction "-"
- Division "/"
- Multiplication "*"
- Remainder "%"

A detailed description of these operators:

- Addition Operator "+"

This operator is used to perform addition or sum function between two operands.

Example:

```
>>> n, v = 25, 69

>>> n + v
```

Your console will print "94", in this case.

- Subtraction Operator "+"

This operator is used to take the first operand and subtracts the second operand from the first one.

Example:

```
>>> n, v = 69, 25
```

```
>>> n - v
```

Your console will print "44", in this case.

- Division Operator "/"

This operand takes the second operand and divides the first operand on the second operand, and gives quotient, as your output.

Example:

```
>>> n, v = 4, 2
>>> n / v
```

Your console will print "2.0", in this case.

- Multiplication Operator "*"

As explained earlier, this operator performs the multiplication operation between the first operand and the second.

Example:

```
>>> n, v = 4, 2
>>> n * v
```

Your console will print "8", in this case.

- Remainder Operator "%"

This operator is responsible for the operation of division, and it gets the remainder as your output.

Example:

```
>>> n, v = 4, 2
```

```
>>> n % v
```

Your console will print "0", in this case.

- Comparison operator in Python

Comparison operators, in Python, are used to compare two operands and returns a Boolean type, i.e., TRUE or FALSE, respectively.

- ==

True: This operator is used if and only if the values are logically equal and true.

- !=

True: This operator is used when the values are true but unequal.

- <=

True: This operator is used when the first operand is smaller than or equal to the second operand.

- >=

True: This operator is used when your first operand is greater than or equal to the second operand.

- <>

True: This operator is used if and only if the values are not equal.

- >

True: This operator is used when your first operand is greater than the second operand.

- <

True: This operator is used when your first operand is less than the second one.

- Assignment operators in Python

In Python, we use assignment operators to assign the value to the left operand, of the right-side expression.

- =

Frequently, this operator is used to assign the value of the right expression to the left operand.

- +=

This operator is used to build the estimation of the left operand by the estimation of the correct operand and appoint the altered an incentive back to the left operand.

Example:

```
>>> n = 2, v = 4

>>> n += v
```

This will be equivalent to

```
>>> n = n + v

>>> print (n)
```

And your console may print the value if n as "6".

- -=

As far as this operator is concerned, it diminishes the estimation of the left operand by the estimation of the correct operand and dole out the changed an incentive back to the left operand.

Example:

>>> n, v = 4, 2

>>> n -= v

This will be equivalent to

n = n - v

>>>print (n)

And your console may print the value if n as "2".

- *=

It increases the estimation of the left operand by the estimation of the correct operand and appoint the altered an incentive back to the left operand.

Example:

>>> n, v = 4 , 2

>>> a * = b

This will be equivalent to

n = n * v

>>> print (n)

And your console may print the value if n as "8".

- %=

This operator is responsible for Divides the estimation of the left operand by that of the correct operand and appoint the update back to the left operand.

Example:

>>> n, v = 4 , 2

>>> a % = b

This will be equivalent to

n = n % v

>>> print (n)

And your console may print the value if n as "0".

- Logical Operators in Python

As far as our real lives are concerned, sometimes, we have to make tough choices based upon logical data, i.e., true or false. For example, let us say if someone calls you and asks you, "Are you at home?" You would have two choices, "Yes! I am home" or "No! I am not." This would lie under 0 (false) and 1 (true), in programming. This is known as logical data.

In Python, Logical operators are used to evaluate the expressions to obtain some specific decisions. These operators are highly helpful to write any logic reasonably. Here is the list of logical operators with a brief description to build a better understanding with these operators in Python.

Logical Operator Description

- And Operator

If an expression "n" is true, and another expression "m" is true as well, then the result will be true. In any other case, the result will be false.

This table may help you to understand "and operator", in a better way.

n v n and v

True True True

True False False

False True False

False False False

- Or Operator

This will result in false, if and only if both operands are false. Consider an expression "n" is true, and another expression "v" is false, then the result will be true.

This table may help you to understand "and operator", in a better way.

n m n or m

T rue T rue T rue

T rue F alseT rue

F alseT rue T rue

F alseF alseF alse

Data Types

Python Labels

Before we dive into learning all the data types, let's take a side step and discuss labels. Writing code involves naming variables and objects appropriately so that you can understand what you're looking at immediately. Labels, also known as identifiers, are words represent something in such a way that it makes the code easier to read. For instance, if you're talking about a bottle of water in your code, you shouldn't name the variable that represents it as "var1". That tells you nothing and it makes the entire code confusing. You would have to waste a great deal of time until you figure out which variable you're talking about.

Whenever you name your variables, make sure they are well represented by the label and that they are unique. Do not use the same name multiple times or you will confuse yourself, and worse the program itself. Furthermore, you should avoid similar words as well. We learned earlier how important code commenting is, however, if used in combination with proper identifiers you will not have any problems understanding your code. However, you should take note that certain words cannot be used as labels. These words are exceptions because they are part of Python's own library of keywords that are reserved for various commands. You should read the language's documentation in order to learn which words are reserved, however, some of them are: global, while, False, class, import and so on.

Keep in mind that using an IDE or even certain text editors can help you out with writing proper labels. They can't read your mind, but they will tell you whenever you are trying to use a reserved keyword. This is another advantage of using dedicated programming tools. You won't have to keep a sticky note with all the keywords attached to your monitor.

Introduction to Variables

In Python, the variable definition is handled in two steps. The first step is called the initialization and it refers to determining the container which is identified via a label. The second step involves the assignment, which means you attach a value to your variable and therefore determine the type of data it holds. These two steps are actually taken at the same time and the process is more of a theoretical one that you don't really notice. Here's how all of this can be formulated:

```
myVariable = thisValue
```

The two steps we learned are taken through the equal operator. What we have here is called a statement, in this case an assignment statement. When you write code, you should always keep your statements in proper order. Keep in mind that Python processes code by analysing it from the top to bottom and then it starts over. Furthermore, you could write the statements in the same line, however, that would lead to a lot of chaos.

Now that you know what a variable is, let's see how Python is able to determine which data type is assigned to the variable.

Python has this feature called dynamic typing, which means that it is able to automatically determine what kind of variable it is dealing with. So if you assign an integer to a variable, Python automatically knows that the variable has an integer data type. When working with other programming languages, you have to declare what type of data your variable will contain. Therefore, if it's an integer you have to declare it first and then assign an integer value to it. This is another advantage of working with Python. All you have to do is write your code without worrying too much about the details. Let the interpreter do the heavy lifting for you.

Furthermore, if you make the mistake of performing an operation on a data type that is not eligible for that operation, Python will let you know. However, there is one disadvantage when relying on this system. Because you don't have to declare your variable's data type, as a beginner, you might accidentally create a variable when you don't need one, or assign the wrong data type to it. It's not always easy to pay attention to all the variables you created, however, this problem can easily be fixed.

The best practice when writing a program is to declare all of your variables at the beginning of your project. Keep in mind that the program isn't affected by simple assignments because you aren't instructing the interpreter to perform any operation. If you say x is equal to 10 that's all there is to it. It doesn't really mean anything else. However, by keeping all of your eggs in the same basket you will be able to keep track of them. Keep in mind that this doesn't mean you have to come up with all of your variables from the beginning. You can always return to the start of your program and declare them whenever you need to.

Strings

The string is the most basic data type, along with numbers. You have actually already used a string when you wrote your first program. The line of text you printed is considered a string. Simply put, strings are sets of characters that are defined between quotation marks. Keep in mind that text also includes numbers and punctuation marks. Even though numbers are normally classified under their own data types such as integers and floats, if you write them between quotes, they are considered textual characters part of a string.

In your first program you had a single statement that was printed with the print function. Keep in mind that you can also print any number of statements, even in the same line, even if they are represented by several variables. This is done with one of the most popular operations you will perform on strings called concatenation. This concept is simple. All it involves is linking multiple strings together. Here's a simple example:

```
charRace = "human"

charGender = "male"

print  (charRace,     charGender)
```

The output will be "human male".

As you can see, we have two variables and each one of them holds a string. We can print both of them by separating the variables with commas when writing the print statement. Keep in mind that there are multiple ways you can do this. For instance, if you don't want to use variables but you need to concatenate the strings, you can get rid of the commas inside the print statement. You will notice a little problem, though. Here's the example:

```
print ("school" "teacher")
```

The result is "schoolteacher". What happened? We didn't leave any whitespace. Take note that whitespace can be part of a string just as numbers and punctuation marks. If you don't leave a space, words will be glued together. The solution is to simply add one blank space before or after one of the strings, inside the quotes.

Next, let's see what happens if you try to combine the two methods and concatenate a variable together with a simple string.

print (charRace "mage")

This is what you will see:

File "<stdin>", line 1

print (characterGender "warrior")

^ SyntaxError: invalid syntax

Congratulations, you got your first syntax error. What's the problem here? We tried to perform the concatenation without using any kind of separator between the two different items.

Let's take a look at one more method frequently used to concatenate a set of strings. Type the following:

x = "orc"

y = " mage"

x + y

As you can see you can apply a mathematical operator when working with string variables. In this case, we add x to y and achieve string concatenation. This is a simple method and works just fine, however, while you should be aware of it, you shouldn't be using it. Mathematical operations require processing power. Therefore, you are telling your Python program to use some of your computer juice on an operation that could be written in such a way as to not consume any resources. Whenever you work on a project, at least a much more complex one, code optimization becomes one of your priorities and that involves managing the system's resource requirement properly. Therefore, if you have to concatenate a large number of string variables, use the other methods that don't involve any math.

Numbers

Numbers, just like strings, are basic but frequently used no matter how simple or complex your program is. Assigning a number to a variable is done exactly the same as with any other data type. You simply declare it like so:

```
x = 10

y = 1
```

Don't forget that Python will automatically know which data type we're assigning. In this case, it identifies our values as integers. Integers are whole numbers that can be either positive or negative. It cannot contain decimal points.

Another numeric data type we mentioned earlier is the float. This is a float:

```
x = 10.234
```

Floats can be negative or positive numbers but they must have decimal points, otherwise they're just integers.

Finally, we have the third numeric data type, which is the boolean. This type holds only two values. It can either be true or false, or in computer language 1 or 0. Booleans are normally used together with logical operators instead of mathematical operators like integers and floats.

Basic Operators

Now that you know a few data types and got used to working with variables, let's start actually performing some handy operations. Variables that hold integers or floats can be manipulated by using the most basic arithmetic operators. For instance, you can subtract, add, multiply, and divide. Whenever you work with these operators you will create an expression instead of a statement. What does that mean? Expressions are essentially code that has to be processed by the computer system in order to find the value. Let's take a look at some exercises you can play with:

```
apples = 10 + 2

bananas = 10 - 4

pears = 6 * 2

fruit = apples + bananas * pears

fruit

84
```

Did you perhaps forget your elementary math and expected to see 216 as the result? That's probably because you calculate the sum in your head and then multiplied it. However, that's not how this calculation works. Python automatically knows which rules to follow and it processes each operation in the order it is required.

As you can see, Python is capable of evaluating the expression and then deciding which blocks need to be processed before other blocks. This order that the programming language follows is called an operator precedence. Always pay attention to basic mathematical and logical rules because if you don't, Python will. If you had something else in mind for your program for instance, and you wanted the result to be 216, you need to write the operation to reflect that. In order words, you need to calculate the sum first and then multiply it.

In this example we only worked with integers in order to showcase the most basic operators. However, if you would replace them with floats, the same rules apply.

In addition, it's worth mentioning that Python is capable of converting an integer to a float or even to a string. Any number can be converted to an integer by typing "int (n)", or a float by typing "float (n)" or a string by typing str (objectname).

You'll notice that these are functions because they follow the same structure as the print function which you used earlier. Once we declare the function we want to use, we need to place the value or variable or object in between the parentheses in order to manipulate it. Here's how these basic conversions work:

float (13)

Result: 13.0

int (13.4)

Result: 13

Now that you know the basics, you should start practicing on your own. Create a few different variables and think of all the operations you can perform with them. Don't forget that reading is not enough and you should always take the extra time to practice.

Making Your Program Interactive

Because you have learned all these preliminaries, it is now the time to start typing some actual code and run them interactively on your python program. Note that you had already started typing in the python interactive session by typing two lines of information text that not only gave the Python version number but also a few hints as illustrated in our early discussion. Usually, the result of our code will be displayed below the input lines when we work interactively and this is after pressing the Enter key. When you type the print statement at the prompt, for example, a Python string also called output will echo back right away. Therefore, there is no need of creating a source code file or run the code a compiler if you are not using Python language. Later, you will learn how to run multiline statements and such statements run as soon as they are entered in their lines and press Enter button twice.

Reasons for the Interactive Prompt

Even though the interactive prompt will echo the results when you run it, it will not save the code in the file. This shows that you cannot handle the bulk of coding in the interactive sessions as you may think. The interactive prompt has turned out to be a good place to test program files or experiment the language on the fly.

Experimenting

Due to its ability to execute the code immediately, the interactive prompt has become the best place to experiment with language. It will be used to illustrate some smaller experiments in this book later. If you are not sure about the working of python code, you can see what takes place when you ire up the interactive command line. If you are reading code in the Python program, for example, you may see an expression that you do not understand its meaning. Example of such expressions could be 'Spam!'*8. You will spend a lot of your time reading the manuals, or books, or even search over the internet to see its meaning.

With immediate response you will receive at the interactive prompt, you can use it to quickly determine the working of the code. From here, for instance, it is clear that code does string repetition. The sign '*' is used in Python to mean the multiplication of numbers as well as repetition for the strings. It is just like concatenating the strings to themselves repeatedly. You will not break anything by this experiment. Generally, Python code is the most appropriate to run as it does not result in the deletion of the files.

Moreover, it is an error to use a variable that has not been assigned value in Python programming. Some errors can go undetected if you fill the names in with defaults. Therefore, to do away with such errors, it is important to start initial counters from zero before adding anything to them and also make sure you have initial lists to help you extend them properly. With initial lists and counting from zero, you will be able to run your program without producing any error

Testing

In addition to serving as a tool or experimenting, the interactive interpreter is used to test the code you will be writing in the files while learning the

Python language. In fact, we will show you how to import the module files interactively. Also, we will show you how to run the tests on the tools defined by typing calls at the interactive prompt.

Additionally, many programmers test programming components at the interactive prompt. As a programmer you can import, test, and run functions and classes in the Python files regardless of their sources. This is achieved by typing calls to linked-in-C functions as well as exercising Java classes in Python. Finally, with the interactive nature of the Python, it is able to support an experimental programming style thus making it convenient for you to get started. This is making the Python programming to be simple, easy, and best for beginners to use to run the code on their programs.

Guidelines for using the Interactive Prompt Effectively

Even though it is easy to use interactive prompt, as a beginner, there are many things you should consider when using it to ensure your code runs without producing errors. The following guidelines will help you to avoid making common mistakes seen by other beginners. Just take your time to read them:

- Ensure you only type Python command.

In many cases, beginners make a big mistake by typing system commands in the interactive prompt. This makes their computer to display errors when they try to run their programs. Even though there are many different ways of running system commands from the python code, these methods do not involve typing the commands themselves as you will see in this book.

- Only use print statements in the files

After seeing that interactive interpreter prints the results of an expression automatically, there is no need for you to complete typing print statements in the interactive python. Although interactive interpreter is a nice feature, it sometimes confuses many programmers particularly the beginners when writing code in the files as they must use print statements to make sure that their results are not automatically echoed.

- Avoid indenting at the interactive prompt

Whether you are typing into a text file or interactively, it is important to make sure that all your untested statements start all the way to the left in column 1. In case you don't follow the above instruction, Python will print syntax error since the black space of your code will be taken as indentation for grouping nested statements. Remember that a leading space will always generate an error message if you start with tab or space at the interactive prompt.

- Make sure you note all prompt changes

These changes are essential for compound statements. Although we will not be working with compound /multiline statements at the moment, it is important to know that typing line 2 of a compound statement interactively can make the prompt to change automatically.

- Make sure that the compound statements are terminated at the interactive prompt that has a blank line.

A blank line plays a vital role in Python programming as it tells interactive python a programmer has completed typing the multiline statement and you only need to press the Enter button twice. However, it is not a must to use it in a file. You can ignore them if they are present.

Entering Multiline Statements

Most of the beginners do not know how to enter multiline statements in the Python program. For instance, last week, we received many emails and messages from the students across the world looking or clarification about entering compound statements. Though it sounds like a hard thing, it is the easiest things to handle with the Python programming languages. To help you understand this, we will introduce compound statements and discuss their syntax in details.

Since they have different behavior or their behavior differs at the interactive prompt and in the file, the following steps are essential for anyone entering multiline statements. Terminate all the compound statements including those for loops and test if there are blank lines at the interactive prompt. Similarly, you can terminate all compound statements before running it by pressing the Enter button twice.

System Command Lines

Even though you can use an interactive prompt to carry out testing and experimenting of your python code, one of the issues associated with it is that your programs disappear immediately they are executed by the Python interpreter. We cannot run the code we have already typed without retyping it since it is not stored in a file. We only need to retype it from scratch or we can cut-and-paste it. However, to carry out this process effectively, we will have to edit out the python prompt and program outputs.

Additionally, we can save our programs permanently by writing our codes in the files, popularly called modules. Modules refer to simple text files that contain python statements. After coding, we will be able to ask the Python interpreter to execute the statement in various ways such as system command lines, file icon clicks, and IDLE user interface. It will execute our code from bottom in a module file every time we run the files. There are many terminologies used in this domain. In Python, for example, module files are called programs. In other words, a program is seen as a series of pre-coded statements in a file executed repeatedly. Sometimes, module files run directly are called scripts, a term that is used to formerly mean a top-level program file in Python. Also, some programmers use the term module to mean a file imported from another file. We will see how these terms are used later in this book.

No matter how you call them, we will explore different ways of running code that are typed into the module files. We will concentrate on the basic ways of running the files. This will involve listing names in a python command line entered at the system prompt o our computer. Although this can be avoided using a GU such as IDLE as we will see later, a system shell and text editor window constitute more integrated development environment, thus providing programmers with direct control over their programs.

First Script

Make sure you have a conducive environment, that is, there is no disturbance before we start working on our first project now. To get started, let us open up our favorite text editor, either the IDLE editor or Notepad and type the following words in the new text file called scrpt1.spy, and then save them in our working code directory that we had set earlier.

Note

We have added some formal Python comments, including text after the #characters. This is necessary in Python as it makes the lines formal by themselves. Also, you should know that the text after # is always seen as a human-readable comment, and as such not considered to be part of the syntax statements. Therefore, there will be no impact to ignore these comments if you are copying the code because they are informative.

How to Run Files with Command Lines

After saving the text file, it is now the time to ask the Python to run the file. This is achieved by listing its file name and we will do it as the first argument to the Python command just like it is done at the system shell prompt. Remember, you can type a system shell command in your preferred system like an xterm window or a window command prompt to provide command-line entry. However, ensure you run it at the system prompt. Also, make sure you replace the term, 'python' with a full directory path just like we did when our PATH setting was not configured. By replacing it, the system will successfully run your program.

Additionally, as a beginner, you should not type any proceeding text in the script 1.py source file created in our last section. The texts include a system command, as well as program output. The first line must be shell command for running the source file in addition to the line.

List, Tuples and dictionaries

Lists

They are exactly as they sound and function pretty much the same. A list, in Python, is represented by square brackets '[]' and it can hold multiple items within it. You can store as many items or values as you like within a list and recall each component easily.

Let us look at a simple list first to see how exactly it works. For that, we have six imaginary volunteers; Joey, Chandler, Ross, Phoebe, Rachel, and Monica. Let's also assume that we have no idea of the obvious connection to these names. Time to create our first list:

```
friends = ["Joey", "Chandler", "Ross", "Phoebe", "Rachel", "Monica"]
```

And we have our list created. Since we are using string values, we will need to use quotation marks to let Python know that these are string values.

Suppose you do not know what's on the list. You do not even know how long the list is. Our target is to find out:

- The number of components within this list
- Value of individual components

To do that, we will first need to see how long the list is, and we can do just that by using the len() function. The len() function basically displays the length of characters, components or items within a variable or a list.

```
friends = ["Joey", "Chandler", "Ross", "Phoebe", "Rachel", "Monica"]

print(len(friends))
```

Output:

6

Now, we have obtained one piece of information. Moving to the next one, let us find out what is at the start of this list. To do that, we will call up the first element, and this is where the concept of index position comes in.

An index is the position of a component. Here, the first component is 'Joey' and to find out that, we will do this:

```
friends = ["Joey", "Chandler", "Ross", "Phoebe", "Rachel", "Monica"]

print(friends)
```

Here, we will use the square brackets and use the value of zero. Why zero and not one? In Python, and in quite a few languages as well, the first position is always a zero. Here, "friends" essentially tells the program to print the component with the first index position. The output, obviously, is:

Joey

Similarly, let's print the rest out accordingly!

```
friends = ["Joey", "Chandler", "Ross", "Phoebe", "Rachel", "Monica"]

print(friends)

print(friends)

print(friends)

print(friends)

print(friends)

print(friends)
```

Output:

```
Joey

Chandler

Ross

Phoebe

Rachel

Monica
```

There is another way to do this. Suppose you do not know the length of the list, and you wish to print out the last recorded entry of the same, you can do that by using the following method:

```
friends = ["Joey", "Chandler", "Ross", "Phoebe", "Rachel", "Monica"]

print(friends[-1])
```

Output:

Monica

The '-1' will always fetch you the last entry. If you use '-2' instead, it will print out the second to last entry as shown here:

```
friends = ["Joey", "Chandler", "Ross", "Phoebe", "Rachel", "Monica"]

print(friends[-2])
```

Output:

Rachel

There are other variations involved here, as well. You can call the items from a specific starting point. Using the same list above, let's assume we wish the prompt to print out the last three entries only. We can do that easily by using the starting index number of the value we wish to print. In this case, it would be the index number '3':

```
friends = ["Joey", "Chandler", "Ross", "Phoebe", "Rachel", "Monica"]

print(friends[3:])
```

Output:

['Phoebe', 'Rachel', 'Monica']

You can also limit what you wish to see on the screen further by setting a range of index numbers. The first number, the one before the colon, represents the starting point. The number that you input after the colon is the end point. In our list of friends, we have a range from zero to five, let us narrow our results down a little:

```
friends = ["Joey", "Chandler", "Ross", "Phoebe", "Rachel", "Monica"]

print(friends[2:5])
```

Output:

['Ross', 'Phoebe', 'Rachel']

Remember, the last index number will not be printed; otherwise, the result would have also shown the last entry.

You can modify the values of a list quite easily. Suppose you wish to change the entry at index number five of the above list, and you wish to change the entry from 'Monica' to 'Geller,' this is how you would do so:

```
friends = ["Joey", "Chandler", "Ross", "Phoebe", "Rachel", "Monica"]

friends = "Geller"

print(friends)
```

Output:

['Joey', 'Chandler', 'Ross', 'Phoebe', 'Rachel', 'Geller']

It is that easy! You can use lists with loops and conditional statements to iterate over random elements and use the ones which are most suitable to the situation. Practice a little and you should soon get the hang of them.

What about if you wish to add numbers or values to the existing lists? Do we have to scroll all the way up and continue adding numbers manually? No! There are things called methods, which you can access at any given time to carry out various operations.

Here's a screen grab to show just how many options you have available to you once you press the '.' Key:

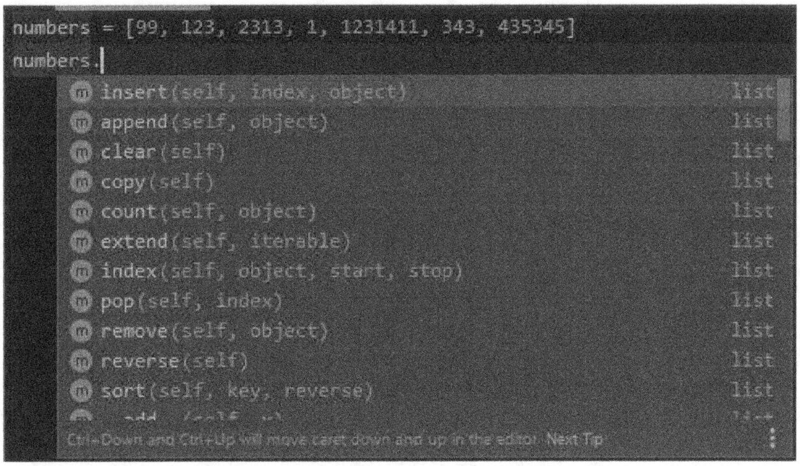

We will not be talking about all of these, but we will briefly look at some basic methods that every programmer should know.

Straight away, the 'append' method is what we use to add values. Simply type in the name of the list you wish to recall, followed by ".append" to let the program know you wish to add a value. Type in the value and that is it!

The problem with using the append method is that it adds the item randomly. What if you wish to add a value to a specific index number? To do that, you will need to use the insert method.

Using an insert method, you will need to do this:

```
numbers = [99, 123, 2313, 1, 1231411, 343, 435345]

numbers.insert(2, 999)

print(numbers)
```

Output:

```
[99, 123, 999, 2313, 1, 1231411, 343, 435345]
```

The number was added right where I wanted. Remember to use an index position that is valid. If you are unsure, use the len() function to recall how many components are within a list. That should then allow you to know the index positions available.

You can also remove items from a list as well. Simply use the remove() method and input the number/value you wish to remove. Please note that if your list has more than one values that are exactly the same, this command will only remove the first instance only.

Let us assume you are presented with a list of mixed entries. There is no order that they follow. The numbers are just everywhere, disregarding the order. If you wish, you can sort the entire list to look more appealing by using the sort() method.

```
numbers = [99, 123, 2313, 1, 1231411, 99, 435345]

numbers.sort()

print(numbers)
```

Output:

```
[1, 99, 99, 123, 2313, 435345, 1231411]
```

You know, you can also have it the other way around by using the reverse() method. Try it!

To completely empty a list, you can use the clear() method. This specific method will not require you to pass any argument as a parameter. There are other methods such as pop() (which takes away the last item on the list only) that you should experiment with. Do not worry, it will not crash your system down or expose it to threats. The IDE is like a safe zone for programmers to test out various methods, programs, and scripts. Feel free and feel at ease when charting new waters.

Tuples

As funny as the name may be, tuples are pretty much like lists. The only major difference is that these are used when you really do not wish for certain specialized values to change at all throughout the program. Once you create a tuple, it cannot be modified or changed later on.

Tuples are represented by parenthesis (). If you try and access the methods, you will no longer have access to the methods that you did when you were using lists. These are secure and used only in situations where you are certain you do not wish to change, modify, add or remove items. Normally, we will be using lists, but it is great to know we have a safe way to do things as well.

Dictionaries

Unlike tuples and lists, dictionaries are different. To begin with, they work with "key value pairs" which sounds confusing, I know. However, let us look at what exactly a dictionary is and how we can call, create and modify the same.

To help us with the explanation, we have our imaginary friend here named James who has graciously accepted to volunteer for the exercise. We then took some information from him such as his name, email, age, the car he drives, and we ended up with this information:

Name - James

Age - 58

Email - james@domain.com

Car - Tesla T1

What we have here are called key pairs. To represent the same within a dictionary, all we need is to create one. How do we do that? Let's have a look.

```
friend = {
"name": "James",
"age": 30,
"email": "james@domain.com",
"car": "Tesla T1"
}
```

We define a dictionary using {} braces. Add each pair as shown above with a colon in the middle. Use a comma to separate items from one another. Now, you have a dictionary called 'friend' and you can access the information easily.

Now, to call up the email, we will use square brackets as shown here:

```
friend = {
"name": "James",
"age": 30,
"email": "james@domain.com",
"car": "Tesla T1"
}
```

```
print(friend["email"])
```

Output:

james@domain.com

Similarly, try recalling the other elements to try it out yourself. Once again, I remind you that Python is case sensitive. If you recall 'age' as 'Age', it will not work at all.

Suppose you wish to recall an item without knowing the key pairs within a dictionary. If you type in a key named 'dob', the program is going to return an error like this:

```
Traceback (most recent call last):
  File "C:/Users/Programmer/PycharmProjects/PFB/Lists2.py", line 7, in <module>
print(friend["dob"])
KeyError: 'dob'
```

There is a way you can check for values without the program screaming back at you with red/pink fonts. Use the .get() method instead and the program will simply say 'None,' which represents the absence of value.

You can also give any keypair, that may not have existed before, a default value as well.

```
friend = {
"name": "James",
"age": 30,
"email": "james@domain.com",
"car": "Tesla T1"
}
print(friend.get("dob", "1, 1, 1900"))
```

Output:

1, 1, 1900

Unlike tuples, you can actually add, modify or change values within a dictionary. I have already shown you how to do that with lists, but just for demonstration purposes, here's one way you can do that.

```
friend["age"] = 60
print(friend["age"])
```

Output:

60

Now, that wasn't so bad, was it? This then ends our trip to the world of lists, tuples, and dictionaries. It is vital that you pay close attention to these as you will be needing to use a few of them, if not all at once, more often than you might imagine. The more you practice and familiarize yourself with lists, tuples, and dictionaries, the easier it will be to create some incredible programs and code in efficient codes at the same time.

Functions and Modules

Why use modules?

Modules allow us to organize the elements and components inside our codes in an easier way, providing us with a big package of variables that are auto contained. Names that are defined on a superior level in a module file automatically will become an attribute of the object of the imported module.

Another advantage of using modules is that they let us reuse the code, using data services and linking individual files to broaden our program.

The main reason why we think that the modules are a very useful tool when it comes to programming is that they are really helpful to organize and reuse our code. This is very important when we talk about OOP (Object-Oriented Programming) since on that mode, the modularization and reusage are very popular. Since Python is a programming language oriented for that, it comes very user-friendly.

Imagine that you want to create an application or a program, more complex than what we have been doing until now. For it, you are going to need one of the previous codes to complement. Here is when you see the real benefit of the modules since you will be able to simply add one of the old codes to the complex application you want to do.

In modules, we will also have modularization. It is based on dividing our codes into several tiny pieces of codes, so that, at the moment of making the complex program or application, it won't have hundreds and hundreds of lines of codes that could be annoying and hard to read. Instead, the code will be separated into tiny files.

How create a module on Python

Creating a module is something very easy that anyone can do, all that needs to be done is to create a file with the .py extension, then, that file will be stored on a folder of your preference; this is known as import.

In case we want to create a module of our own, you will have to do the following. We will make a program on which we will create a module that could be used later.

The module syntax is as follows:

As you could see, the syntax is really simple, since it is pretty much like creating a function. After we created it, we must be able to import it from another program, in order to do that, we will use the import statement.

Import statement and module

Import Statement

A module is able to contain definitions of a function and even statements, which can be executable. With this, it is possible to initialize a module since they execute only when our module is on the import statement.

Modules are capable of importing other modules, that is why people use to put the import type statements at the beginning of each since with the names of our imported modules, they will locate on a space named global; function that modules have for importing.

With the help of the last example, we can manage to import the module created previously and use the functions that we defined there.

As you see in this example, we created the op variable, who takes the task of storing a string, which will specify the option that the users choose. Then, two variables would be initialized, a and b; they will store the value of the operators we are going to use to perform the mathematical operations.

Afterward, the result variable will store the value that the function calculator returns, according to the operators and the type of operation that the users want. The function calculator comes from the module that we have imported.

When the Python interpreter finds the import statement, it imports the module, as long as it is located on the full search path. The search path is nothing but a list where all the directories that Python accesses before importing any module are located.

How to Import a Module?

For being able to import a module, we just have to follow some instructions and steps that are performed at the moment of the execution:

We look for the module through the module search path, compile to byte code, and lastly, we execute the byte-code of our module to then build an object that defines it.

How can I search for a module through Search Path?

To search for a module, our search system compounds of the concatenation of paths; these can be seen on the directory "Home" of our program. After this, the environment PYTHONPATH will be located from left to right, and that is how we will find the directory of default libraries.

Namespaces in Modules

As you know, modules are files. Python creates a module object in which all the names that we assigned in that module-file will be contained. What does that mean? This means that namespaces are just places where all the names that later become attributes are created.

What Are the Attributes?

Attributes are the names that have been assigned to a value considered of a higher level on a module file, which does not belong to

a function or class.

Calling a function in python;

A function that has been defined will only set the parameters for it and then give it its name.

At the point in time that you have set the structure for the block of code, you are going to be able to execute it by creating another function or by using Python directly in a prompt that is provided by the program.

Example

#! / usr/ bin/ python

#the definition for my function is going to entered in here

Def printme (str) :

"This will be where the string is printed"

Print str

Return;

at this point I am going to be able to call upon the printme function

Printme ("This will be where the first definition is going to go")

Printme ("This is the second definition")

Output

This will be where the first definition is going to go.

This is the second definition.

Value vs Pass by reference

When a parameter is set in Python, it has to be passed by a reference.

This means that if you are wanting to change the parameter, any change that you end up making is going to be reflected back to the function that has been called.

Example

#!/ usr/ bin/ python

#define your function in this space

Def nameme (asection) :

"This is going to be before you change anything"

Asection. Append ([5, 10, 15, 20]);

Print "the numbers in the function I created: " , asection

Return

#here is where you are going to change your function

Asection = [2, 4, 6];

Nameme(asection) ;

Print "Any number that is not in the function " , asection

Output

Numbers in the function [2, 4, 6, [5, 10, 15, 20]]

Numbers not in the function [2, 4, 6, [5, 10, 15, 20]]

Argument functions

There are four types of arguments that are going to be used with functions

Variable-length arguments

Required arguments

Default arguments

Keyword arguments

Required

Arguments are going to be sent through the function in the order in which the arguments are in order. It is known as a required argument.

There are various other arguments that can be used, however, the argument that you pick needs to match the definition of the function exactly or you are going to end up with an error from Python.

When you are calling upon a function, you have to ensure that it passes at least one argument or else you will end up with a error that is syntax based.

Example

```
#!/ usr/ bin / python

#definition of the function belongs here

Def nameme ( str )

"This will be the string that is written inside of the function"

Print str

Return ;

#this will be where the function is called upon

Nameme( )
```

Because no argument has been listed, you are going to end up receiving an error and having to go back and fix your code.

Keyword

Keyword arguments are going to function like when a function is called upon.

The keyword argument is going to be defined by the name of the parameter.

Thanks to this argument, you are going to be able to skip arguments or put them in a different order since the interpreter is going to be able to look at the keywords and then match it with the parameter that it needs to be placed with.

Example

```
#!/ usr/ bin / python
```

#definition of the function

Def nameme (str) :

"The string is going to be printed here"

Print str

Return ;

#the function can now be called upon here

Nameme (str – "A section ")

Output

A section

You are going to be able to put your parameters where you want them without worrying about getting an error message.

Example

#! / usr/ bin / python

#definition of the function belongs here

Def printdata (title, years of service) :

"The data that is put into the function has to be passed through this"

Print "title: " , title

Print "years of service " , years of service

Return ;

#the function can now be called upon

Printdata (years of service = 5, title = associate

Output

Title: associate

Years of service: 5

Defaults

Values that are not given inside of the function are going to fall back on a value that Python has deemed the default value.

Example

#!/ usr / bin / python

#define your function in this section

Def printdata (title, years of service = 5) :

"The data has to be passed through this function"

Print "title : " , title

Print "years of service " , years of service

Return ;

#here is where the function will be called

Printdata (years of service = 15, title = "associate")

Printdata (title = "associate")

Output

Title: associate

Years of service 5

Title: associate

Years of service 15

Functions for globals ( ) and locals ( )

These functions are going to be used so that the global and local namespaces are returned but it is going to depend the location in which they are located.

When you are working with the local ( ) function, it will give you the names that are in the function for that particular location.

A globals ( ) function is going to return the names for the function in that global location.

There is a dictionary that has all of the types for both of the functions listed. Names are going to be pulled with the keys ( ) function.

Function reload ( )

Any imported module is going to be carried out once.

Should you want to make the module be executed again, you are going to use the function reload ( ).

This function is going to reload the module that was previously imported.

Syntax

Reload(module_name)

The module name is going to be what the module is named in the Python directory. The string name is not going to be name that is placed in this space.

Example

Reload(South)

Python Packages

There is a hierarchy when it comes to the file directory and this is going to end up defining applications that are in Python.

This package will have sub-subpackages, subpackages, and modules.

Working with Files

The Python programming language allows us to work on two different levels when we refer to file systems and directories. One of them is through the module os, which facilitates us to work with the whole system of files and directories, at the level of the operating system itself.

The second level is the one that allows us to work with files, this is done by manipulating their reading and writing at the application level, and treating each file as an object.

In python as well as in any other language, the files are manipulated in three steps, first they are opened, then they are operated on or edited and finally they are closed.

What is a file?

A python file is a set of bytes, which are composed of a structure, and within this we find in the header, where all the data of the file is handled such as, for example, the name, size and type of file we are working with; the data is part of the body of the file, where the written content is handled by the editor and finally the end of the file, where we notify the code through this sentence that we reach the end of the file. In this way, we can describe the structure of a file.

The structure of the files is composed in the following way:

- File header: These are the data that the file will contain (name, size, type)

- File Data: This will be the body of the file and will have some content written by the programmer.

- End of file: This sentence is the one that will indicate that the file has reached its end.

Our file will look like this:

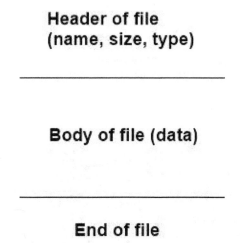

Header of file
(name, size, type)

Body of file (data)

End of file

How can I access a file?

There are two very basic ways to access a file, one is to use it as a text file, where you proceed line by line, the other is to treat it as a binary file, where you proceed byte by byte.

Now, to assign a variable a file type value, we will need to use the function open (), which will allow us to open a file.

Open() function

To open a file in Python, we have to use the open() function, since this will receive the name of the file and the way in which the file will be opened as parameters. If the file opening mode is not entered, it will open in the default way in a read-only file.

We must keep in mind that the operations to open the files are limited because it is not possible to read a file that was opened only for writing, you cannot write to a file which has been opened only for reading.

The open () function consists of two parameters:

- It is the path to the file we want to open.

- It is the mode in which we can open it.

Its syntax is as follows:

```
function = open("file.txt", "w")
function.write()
function.close()
```

Of which the parameters:

File: This is an argument that provides the name of the file we want to access with the open() function, this is what will be the path of our file.

The argument file is considered a fundamental argument, since it is the main one (allowing us to open the file), unlike the rest of the arguments which can be optional and have values that are already predetermined.

Mode: The access modes are those that are in charge of defining the way in which the file is going to be opened (it could be for reading, writing, editing).

There are a variety of access modes, these are:

r	This is the default open mode. Opens the file for reading only
r+	This mode opens the file for its reading and writing
rb	This mode opens the file for reading only in a binary format
w	This mode opens the file for writing only. In case the file does not exist, this mode creates it
w+	This is similar to the w mode, but this allows the file to be read
wb	This mode is similar to the w mode, but this opens the file in a binary format
wb+	This mode is similar to the wb mode, but this allows the file to be read
a	This mode opens a file to be added. The file starts writing from the end
ab	This is similar to mode a, but opens the file in a binary format
a+	This mode is pretty much like the mode a, but allows us to read the file.

In summary, we have three letters, or three main modes: r,w and a. And two submodes, + and b.

In Python, there are two types of files: Text files and plain files. It is very important to specify in which format the file will be opened to avoid any error in our code.

Read a file:

There are three ways to read a file:

1. read([n])

2. readlines()

3. readline([n])

Surely at this point, we have the question of what is meant by the letter n enclosed in parentheses and square brackets? It's very simple, the letter n is going to notify the bytes that the file is going to read and interpret.

Read method ([ ])

```
myfile = open("D:\\pythonfile\\mypythonfile.txt","r")
myfile.read(9)
```

There we could see that inside the read() there is a number 9, which will tell Python that he has to read only the first nine letters of the file

Readline(n) Method

The readline method is the one that reads a line from the file, so that the read bytes can be returned in the form of a string. The readline method is not able to read more than one line of code, even if the byte n exceeds the line quantity.

Its syntax is very similar to the syntax of the read() method.

```
myfile = open("D:\\pythonfile\\mypythonfile.txt","r")
myfile.readline()
```

Readlines(n) Method

The readlines method is the one that reads all the lines of the file, so that the read bytes can be taken up again in the form of a string. Unlike the readline method, this one is able to read all the lines.

Like the read() method and readline() its syntax are very similar:

```
myfile = open("D:\\pythonfile\\mypythonfile.txt","r")
myfile.readlines()
```

Once we have opened a file, there are many types of information (attributes) we could get to know more about our files. These attributes are:

File.name: This is an attribute that will return the name of the file.

File.mode: This is an attribute that will return the accesses with which we have opened a file.

file.closed: This is an attribute that will return a "True" if the file we were working with is closed and if the file we were working with is still open, it will return a "False".

Close() function

The close function is the method by which any type of information that has been written in the memory of our program is eliminated, in order to proceed to close the file. But that is not the only way to close a file; we can also do it when we reassign an object from one file to another file.

The syntax of the close function is as follows:

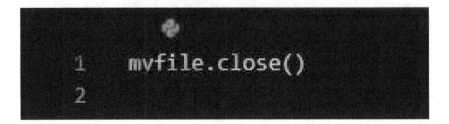

```
mvfile.close()
```

What's a buffer?

We can define the buffer as a file which is given a temporary use in the ram memory; this will contain a fragment of data that composes the sequence of files in our operating system. We use buffers very often when we work with a file which we do not know the storage size.

It is important to keep in mind that, if the size of the file were to exceed the ram memory that our equipment has, its processing unit will not be able to execute the program and work correctly.

What is the size of a buffer for? The size of a buffer is the one that will indicate the available storage space while we use the file. Through the function: io.DEFAULT_BUFFER_SIZE the program will show us the size of our file in the platform in a predetermined way.

We can observe this in a clearer way:

```
import io
    print("Default buffer size:"io.DEFAULT_BUFFER_SIZE)
    file= open("Myfile.txt", mode= "r", buffering=6)
    print(file.line_buffering)
file_contents=file.buffer
for line in file_contents
    print(line)
```

Errors

In our files, we are going to find a string (of the optional type) which is going to specify the way in which we could handle the coding errors in our program.

Errors can only be used in txt mode files.

These are the following:

Ignore_errors()	This will avoid the comments with a wrong or unknown format
Strict_errors()	This is going to generate a subclass or UnicodeError in case that any mistake or fail comes out in our code file

Encoding

The string encoding is frequently used when we work with data storage and this is nothing more than the representation of the encoding of characters, whose system is based on bits and bytes as a representation of the same character.

This is expressed as follows:

```
string.encode(encoding="UTF-8", errors= "strict")
```

Newline

The Newline mode is the one that is going to control the functionalities of the new lines, which can be '\r', " ", none, '\n', and '\r\n'.

The newlines are universal and can be seen as a way of interpreting the text sequences of our code.

1.The end-of-line sentence in Windows: "\r\n".

2.The end-of-line sentence in Max Os: "\r".

3.The end-of-line sentence in UNIX: "\n"

On input: If the newline is of the None type, the universal newline mode is automatically activated.

Input lines can end in "\r", "\n" or "\r\n" and are automatically translated to "\n" before being returned by our program. If their respective legal parameters when coding are met, the entry of the lines will end only by the same given string and their final line will not be translated at the time of return.

On output: If the newline is of the None type, any type of character "\n" that has been written, will be translated to a line separator which we call "os.linesep".

If the newline is of the type " " no type of translator is going to be made, and in case the newline meets any value of which are considered the legal for the code, they will be automatically translated to the string.

Example of newline reading for " ".

```
string.encode(mode="r", newline= " ")
```

Example of newline reading for none:

```
string.encode(mode="w", newline= "none")
```

Manage files through the "os" module

The "os" module allows us to perform certain operations, these will depend on an operating system (actions such as starting a process, listing files in a folder, end process and others).

There are a variety of methods with the "os" module which allow us to manage files, these are:

os.makedirs()	This method of the "os" module will create a new file
os.path.getsize()	This method of the "os" module will show the size of a file in bytes.
os.remove(file_name)	This method of the "os" module will delete a file or the program
os.getcwd ()	This method of the "os" module will show us the actual directory from where we will be working
os.listdir()	This method of the "os" module will list all the content of any folder of our file

os.rename (current_new)	This method of the "os" module will rename a file
os.path.isdir()	This method of the "os" module will transfer the parameters of the program to a folder
os.chdir()	This method of the "os" module will change or update the direction of any folder or directory
os.path.isfile()	This method of the "os" module will transform a parameter into a file.

Xlsx files: xlsx files are those files in which you work with spreadsheets, how is this? Well, this is nothing more than working with programs like Excel. For example, if we have the windows operating system on our computer, we have the advantage that when working with this type of files, the weight of it will be much lighter than other types of files.

The xlsx type files are very useful when working with databases, statistics, calculations, numerical type data, graphics and even certain types of basic automation.

Object Oriented Programming

When we talk about object-oriented programming, we naturally think of process-oriented programming. Process-oriented programming is to analyze the steps to solve the problem, and then use functions to implement these steps one by one when using different methods.

Object-oriented programming is to decompose the problem-solving entities into multiple objects, and the purpose of establishing objects is not to complete one by one but to describe the behavior of things in the process of solving the whole problem.

The following is an example of gobang to illustrate the difference between process-oriented and object-oriented programming.

First, use the process-oriented paradigm:

1. Start the game

2. Player 1 plays first

3. Draw the picture

4. Judges the result

5. Player 2 turn

6. Draw the picture

7. Judges the result

8. Return to Step 2

9. Output Final Results

The above steps are implemented by functions respectively, and the problem is solved using a process-oriented paradigm.

Object-oriented design solves the problem from another way of thinking. When using object-oriented thinking to realize gobang, the whole gobang game can be divided into three types of objects, as follows.

1. Black and White Parties: This represents the two players

2. Chessboard system: This is responsible for drawing pictures

3. Rule system: This is responsible for judging things such as foul, winning or losing, etc.

Among the above three-class objects, the first-class object (black and white parties) is responsible for receiving the user's input and notifying the second-class object (chessboard system) to draw pieces on the chessboard, while the third-class object (rule system) judges the chessboard.

Object-oriented programming ensures the unity of functions, thus making the code easier to maintain.

For example, if we want to add the function of chess now in a process-oriented paradigm, then a series of steps of input, judgment, and display needs to be changed. Even the loops between steps need to be adjusted on a large scale, which is very troublesome.

If object-oriented development is used, only the chessboard object needs to be changed. The chessboard object saves the chessboard scores of both black and white parties, and only needs simple backtracking, without changing the display and rules. At the same time, the calling sequence of the whole object function will not change, and its changes are only partial. Thus, compared with process-oriented, object-oriented programming is more convenient for later code maintenance and function expansion.

Classes and objects

In object-oriented programming, the two most important core concepts are class and object. Objects are concrete things in real life. They can be seen and touched. For example, the book you are holding is an object.

Compared with objects, classes are abstract, which is a general designation for a group of things with the same characteristics and behaviors. For example, when I was a child, my mother said to me, "Son, you should take that kind of person as an example!" The type of people here refers to a group of people who have excellent academic results and who are polite. They have the same characteristics, so they are called "same type" people.

Relationship between Class and Object

As the saying goes, "people are grouped by category, and things are grouped by group," we collectively refer to the collection of things with similar characteristics and behaviors as categories, such as animals, airplanes, etc.

For example, the toy model can be regarded as a class and each toy as an object, thus the relationship between the toy model and the toy can be regarded as the relationship between the class and the object. Class is used to describe the common features of multiple objects and is a template for objects. An object is used to describe individuals in reality. It is an instance of a class. As can be seen, objects are created according to classes, and one class can correspond to multiple objects.

Definition of Class

In daily life, to describe a kind of category, it is necessary to explain its characteristics as well as its uses. For example, when describing such entities as human beings, it is usually necessary to give a definition or name to such things. Human characteristics include height, weight, sex, occupation, etc. Human behaviors include running, speaking, etc. The combination of human characteristics and behaviors can completely describe human beings.

The design idea of an object-oriented program is based on this design, which includes the features and behaviors of things in classes. Among them, the characteristics of things are taken as the attributes of classes, the behaviors of things are taken as the methods of classes, and objects are an instance of classes. So to create an object, you need to define a class first. The class is composed of 3 parts.

(1) Class Name: The name of the class, whose initial letter must be uppercase, such as Person.

(2) Attribute: used to describe the characteristics of things, for example, people have the characteristics of name, age, etc.

(3) Method: Used to describe the behavior of things, for example, people have behaviors such as talking and smiling.

In Python, you can use the class keyword to declare a class with the following basic syntax format:

Class {Enter the entity here}:

This is property of a class

Method of class

The following is a sample code:

```
class Vehicle:
# attribute
# Method
 def drive(self):
Print ("-drivinf Automobile--")
```

In the above example, the class is used to define a class named Vehicle, in which there is a drive method. As can be seen from the example, the format of the method is the same as that of the function.

The main difference is that the method must explicitly declare a self-parameter and be located at the beginning of the parameter list. Self represents the instance of the class (object) itself, which can be used to refer to the attributes and methods of the object. The specific usage of self will be introduced later with practical application.

Creating Objects from Classes

If a program wants to complete specific functions, classes alone are not enough but also instance objects need to be created according to classes.

In Python programs, you can use the following syntax to create an object:

Object {Enter the entity name here } = Class { Enter the name here} ()

For example, create an object Vehicle of driving class with the following sample code:

```
vehicle = driving()
```

In the above code, vehicle is a variable that can be used to access the properties and methods of the class. To add attributes to an object, you can use the following syntax.

Object {Enter entity here}. New {Enter attribute name} = Value

For example, use vehicle to add the color attribute to an object of driving class.

The sample code is as follows:

vehicle.color = "black"

Next, a complete case is used to demonstrate how to create objects, add attributes and call methods. Look at it and clear all your doubts.

Example Spo

```
# Define Class

class Football:

# kick

def kick(goal):

print ("You scored ..." )

# Foul

def foul(self):

print ("You cheated" )

# creates an object and saves its reference with the variable BMW

Barcelona = Football()
```

```
# Add Attribute Representing Color

Barcelona.color = "blue"

# Call Method

Barcelona.goal()

Barcelona.foul()

# Access Attributes

print(Barcelona.color)
```

In Example, a Football class is defined, two methods kick and foul is defined in the class, then an object Barcelona of football class is created, color attribute is dynamically added and assigned to "blue", then goal () and foul () methods are called in turn, and the value of color attribute is printed out.

Structural Methods and Destructural Methods

In Python programs, two special methods are provided: __init___() and __del (), which are respectively used to initialize the properties of the object and release the resources occupied by the class.

Construction method

In the previous example defining classes, we dynamically added the color attribute to the objects referenced by Barcelona. Just imagine, if you create another Football class object, you need to add attributes in the form of "object name. attribute name". For each object created, you need to add attributes once, which is very troublesome.

To solve this problem, attributes can be set when creating an object. Python provides a construction method with a fixed name of_init_(two underscores begin and two underscores end). When creating an instance of a class, the system will automatically call the constructor to initialize the class.

To make everyone better understand, the following is a case to demonstrate how to use the construction method for initialization.

Example: uses the construction method. py

```
# Define Class

class Football:

# construction method

def___init__(kick):

Color = "blue"
```

```
# Foul

def foul(self):

print ("%s Barcelona color is " (self.color))

# creates an object and saves its reference with the variable car

football = Football()

football.foul()
```

In the example, lines 4-5 re-implemented the_init__() method, adding the color attribute to the Football class and assigning it a value of "blue", and accessing the value of the color attribute in the foul method.

No matter how many Football objects are created, the initial value of the color attribute is "blue" by default. If you want to modify the default value of the property after the object is created, you can set the value of the property by passing parameters in the construction method.

The following is a case to demonstrate how to use the construction method with parameters.

Example: uses the parametric construction method. py

```
# Define Class

class Football:

# construction method

def___init__(kick):

Color = "blue"

# Foul
```

```
def foul(self):

print ("%s Barcelona color is " (self.color))

# creates an object and saves its reference with the variable car

football = Football()

football.foul()

# creates an object and saves its reference with the variable bmw

realmadrid = color ("white")

realmadrid.color()
```

In Example, lines 4 to 5 customize the construction method with parameters, and assign the value of the parameters to the color attribute, ensuring that the value of the color attribute changes with the value received by the parameters, and then still access the value of the color attribute in the toot method.

Destructor Methods

Earlier, we introduced the___init___() method. When an object is created, the Python interpreter will call the___init___() method by default. When deleting an object to release the resources occupied by the class, the Python interpreter calls another method by default, which is the___del___ () method.

Next, a case is used to demonstrate how to use a destructor to release the occupied resources.

example: using destructor. py

```
# Define Class

class Football

 def___init__(team, color, name):

 team.name = name

 team.color = color

 def___del__(team):

 print("______del______")

Realmadrid = team ("white", 1)
```

In Example, a class named Person is defined, the initial values of color and team are set in the___init___() method, a print statement is added in the __del___() method, and then an object of the Person class is created using a custom construction method.

When the program ends, the memory space it occupies will be released.

So, can we release the space manually? Yes, Del statement can be used to delete an object and release the resources it occupies.

Add the following code at the end of Example:

```
del realmadrid

print("_______1_______")
```

￼As you can observe from the results, the program outputs "del" before "1". This is because Python has an automatic garbage collection mechanism. When the Python program ends, the Python interpreter detects whether there is currently any memory space to be freed. If there is a del statement, it will be automatically deleted; if the del statement has been manually called, it will not be automatically deleted.

Conclusion

We have come a long way. In this guide, I explained to you the basics of Python language. Learning to program is like learning another language. It takes a lot of patience, study, application, method, passion and above all perseverance.

What I can suggest is to do as much practice as possible by starting to rewrite the hundreds of examples you find in this guide.

Try to memorize them and when you write the code, say it to yourself, in your mind (open bracket, close round brackets and so on). In the beginning, this helped me a lot to memorize better the various steps needed to write a program even if simple.

It is important not to feel like heroes when a program works but above all you should not be depressed when you cannot find a solution to your programming problems. The network is full of sites and blogs where you can always find a solution.

In this 21st century, we can't forget about the importance of web area and happily, Python is surprisingly flexible in developing business enterprise well-known web solutions. The web applications demanding more speed and electricity can be executed with Python. All types of records driven internet applications can be advanced in Python with maximum power and potential.

Python is a dynamic language and supports particular programming patterns which include object- oriented, aspect-oriented, purposeful and imperative. One of the quality capabilities of the language is natural and better memory management.

Primarily employed like a scripting language, Python gives a high-quality degree of functionality. While it may be used as a standalone application, you can also integrate third birthday party gear and personalize its functionality.

Python is thought for its smooth readability. The center philosophies of the language are simple - simplicity over complexity; beauty over ugliness, express over implicit and other similar aphorisms. The most critical view of the language is "Readability Counts," which means that the syntaxes and codes written the use of Python are clean and neat.

The programming language has a huge library that helps programmers. Python additionally has an open source version referred to as the CPython programming platform. It has a massive community of builders who continuously paintings to upgrade features.

Owing to the ease of handling, Python is a "programmer's language". Moreover, studying the language is very simple. One of the most abundant blessings of Python, except clean and without problems readable codes, is the velocity with which you could code.

Programmers can pass on rapid tune because a couple of levels that aren't necessary can be skipped. Another advantage is that programmers get numerous assist from the Python open source developer community.

The portability characteristic of Python is another certainly one of its primary strengths. Not only can Python run on multiple platforms, however also programmers simplest want to write down a single application to work on all operating systems. It is a pretty adaptable language.

Learning Python is not a tough project, even for beginners. So, take the soar and master Python.

Book Two

PYTHON FOR DATA ANALYSIS

Everything you Need to Know About Data Analysis to Easily Get the Python Intermediate Level.

Introduction

The Python programming language is characterized by an easy to learn and intuitive syntax, making it one of the most widely used and preferred programming languages across the world. According to the TIOBE index, Python is ranked as the third popularly used language in 2019. This ranking takes its usage up even further, implying a two percent increase from the previous year.

Python's popularity can also be traced to the high readability of its syntax and simplicity of use. Readability comes in terms of the syntax being written in clean, regular English. This property makes the program less daunting to code in and allows programmers to pay attention to the business at hand instead of trying to keep up with and remember all the details of the language.

How Python Started

Python programming began at the fingertips of a Dutch programmer, name of Guido Van Rossum. He wrote the program sometime in the latter period of the '80s as a hobby project. Since its release to the public, Python has grown and evolved over time to be one of the most acclaimed, polished, and consistent languages in the world of computer programming.

According to Van Rossum, the conception of Python can be traced to a Christmas weekend in December 1989. He had begun working on his hobby project in his free time to develop an interpreter language—a successor to the ABC programming language to which Van Rossum helped develop. However, when the entire process of development came to an end, Python emerged as nothing short of a complete programming language in itself. Given its somewhat already weird history, the name "Python" draws even more questions to the identity of the programming language. Van Rossum had the Unix and C hackers as the target audience of his program, but more importantly, he was especially keen on the then famous TV sitcom—The Monty Python's Flying Circus. Van Rossum explained that he found the name "Python" not only suitable to his taste but appealing to his target audience, so he ran with it.

Properties of Python Programming Language

Python is a dynamically and implicitly typed language in itself, so you are not required to declare variables while coding. The datatypes in Python are enforced, and its variables are sensitive to case. As a result, VALUE and value are processed as two distinct variable types. Furthermore, there are no set out characters used in terminating statements or commands. Every block of code is specified with an indentation. As such, at the beginning of a block of code, an indent is introduced, and a de-dent is used at the end. Statements that require a level of indentation are terminated using a colon (:). To add comments, the hash (#) is used in each line. For multiple line strings, they are used in multi-line comments. To assign values to variables, the equal to (=) is used, while the double equal to (==) signs are used in testing for equality. Increment and decrement can be performed on values using the operators (+=) and (-=), respectively, with the amount placed on the right-hand side of the operator. Such operations can be performed on strings and several other data types.

What is Data Analysis

Data analysis is basically the use of data analytics tools and methods in respect to achieving business goals.

It is a process in which we; scrutinize, transform and sort unprocessed data in order to generate useful information: this process permits evaluation of data through logical and analytical reasoning.

During data analytics, data is generally collected and inspected. It has several uses. While, analyzing data is: Defining, investigation, purification, removing Na values and other outliers in the data and transforming it to produce useful results. To perform data analysis, one need to know the tools in order to take prerequisite action on data awareness of Python, R, SAS, Apache Spark, Tableau Public, Excel, etc. and more. One needs to be keen on tools for data analysis as KNIME, Open Refine.

Data analysis process also comes under data analytics. This involves,

Data collecting.

Data polishing.

Analysis of data.

Data Interpretation.

The final process embraces you with what the data wishes said.

While figuring out the next step next, in regard to marketing, we use analytics since they insure predicting later numbers. However, in regard to data analysis, the process is performed on the final set of data to comprehend prior engagements. Critically, data analytics and data analysis are a necessity to understanding data and how useful it is when comprehending the later demands. They are used to perform data analysis with an overview of the past.

The two basic principles in analyzing data are; Interpolation and extrapolation. Interpolation is taking a look at the data, based on current data; determine past. Especially, this can be useful when performing market analysis and the like. However, extrapolation is taking the current data and making a brave guess as to how it will be in the coming years. It is extensively used of the two as institutions are highly concerned with the future than the past.

These two methods will be wide in your career whence ensuring you know both of them places one at where programming converges. Data usage has rapidly grown in the recent past as huge amount of data gets gathered in the companies. The data is/or might be related to business customers and application users, visitors or even stakeholders. The data is divided and processed to comprehend, decode, and analyze patterns. Data analytics in itself comprises of various skills and tools. Engaging in quantitative and qualitative techniques for gathering data aims for an outcome that can be maximized for graded efficiency, risk reduction, production increment and continued growth of businesses. These methods vary from company to company depending on their demands.

Specifically, data analysis is a special idea; making a tool that uses technologies as tableau public, KNIME, Open Refine and Rapid Miner among others. These tools are used for exploratory analysis hence this gives insight from the available data by; cleaning, using, transforming, modeling and visualizing the data to provide the outcome.

Necessary skills for becoming a data scientist

These are some skills required to become a data scientist.

1. Education: getting a degree in these courses equips you with the necessary skills for processing and analyzing a large amount of data. Though, getting the degree course, do not guarantee that you are through.

The variety of skills you have learned doing your degree program helps to move into data science.

A research paper can clearly and easily destroy the world of data science. Keeping this in mind, ensure a constancy to keep in touch with the data analytics world. This can enable you perform ahead of your colleagues since you will be familiar with the principles and techniques.

2. R Programming: R is majorly used for data science as it is tailored for the data science demands. R is also used to solve all problems faced in data science.

R is generally less useful than other languages in general-purpose programming situations. It's good for data analytics, not usable for anything else comparable important. For a first language, this makes it not ideal, you'll find that even when able to analyze the data, making programs that will be able to actually use it will be a hard nut to crack. In the long run, one wants to focus on making programs that can reliably use data while patronizing the implications on your data.

3. Python coding: This is a great choice for the data scientists accompanied by Java, Perl, C++ and C. 40% of the users prefer Python

as their primary programming language option according to a survey conducted by O'Reilly.

4. Using Hadoop Platform: It is a huge and strong opportunity to be experienced in Pig or Hive. Being familiar with various cloud tools such as Amazon S3 gives you a high definition.

5. SQL DB/Coding: SQL is a Structured Query Language known popularly as a programming language which can be useful for conducting out various operations like addition, deletion, and extraction of data from the DB. When you utilize it for querying a DB it will provide insight.

6. Apache Spark: This is one of the big and most popular data technologies available. Similar to Hadoop, Apache Spark is a big data computation framework. The use of Apache Spark is more advantageous considering that it is faster than Hadoop.

7. AI and Machine Learning: Machine learning and related techniques such as reinforcement learning, neural networks and adversarial learning, is an area which many data scientists out there are not proficient in.

8. Data Visualization: Regularly, in most cases huge amount of data generated in businesses worldwide. Usually, the large data should be decoded into the right readable format.

9. Data that is not structured: Basically, the unformed data is all the system less contents that do not suit in the DB tables.

10. Intellectually curious nature: Owing to the fact that the field of data science is growing rapidly, a data scientist, should and must be able to enquire questions in the field. Since the scientists spend most of their time gathering and sorting data

11. Business understanding: You are expected to contain great comprehending of your industry, knowing the various business problems facing your institution.

12. Communication Skills: People who can perfectly and coherently read and interpret technical things to non-technical teams like the sales and marketing department. These are the great minded data analysts that organizations are searching. This can yield huge growth in businesses by impacting positively through provision of quality services.

13. Teamwork: You need to be able to work freely and as team with the rest in a company. Working with other company officials is a tool to develop and strategize development plans. You can work with the corporate communication department for marketing purposes. In order to create good products, you will interact with mangers and designers

Python Libraries for Data Analysis

The program is assistance to the developers for creation lstandalone PC games and mobiles. With its huge libraries of 137000, Python assist in many ways.

Some certification programs on social media platforms like blogs and videos are very useful in training. You can find blogs, videos, and other resources online as well. Most critical tasks that need important information in order to be done effectively by the data scientists will require guide information to make important decisions concerning the running of business operations and other critical tasks.

1. NumPy: For data scientists and developers, it is one of the first options for those who know technologies involved in data related things. This

Python package is used for performing scientific computations is registered under the BSD license.

2. Theano: Theano is a very helpful library in pythhelps data scientists to create huge several dimensions arrays in conjunction with computing tasks. Similarly, it is same as TensorFlow only that it is not that effective efficiently. It's primarily involved in the parallel and tasks in relation with distributed computing.

3. Keras: Keras is among the empowering libraries in python. It allows for interaction higher-level neural network. Universally, permits different execution and blends over CPU and GPU.

It ensures and awards a user-friendly surrounding thus, decreasing the force needed for cognitive loads and making available results that need to be achieved by the use of simple APIs.

4. PyTorch: This is among the biggest machine learning libraries in python availed to data scientists, other researchers and analysts. This assists them with computational graph designs characterized by constant change. We are talking about quick tensor computation accelerated via GPU and other hard techniques available.

5. SciPy: This Python library is used by data scientists, developers and also researchers. Occasionally, one may be bewildered between, SciPy stack with the library. Basically, SciPy gives you effectiveness, combination, linear algebra computation packages and also statistics.

6. Pandas: PANDAS is the Python Data Analysis Library. Being a wide not closed library source, it is used for providing analysis tools and data

structures which are high-performance. On the NumPy package, in which its main data structure is Data Frame PANDAS is created.

7. PyBrain: this contains various algorithms created and obtained for; supervised and unsupervised learning, neural network and evolution.

8. SciKit-Learn: mainly, this tool is simply useful for tasks such data analyzing and data mining. It is an open source type of tool which can be used recycled and used by all in dynamic contexts, it is also licensed under BSD

9. Matplotlib: This Python library is usually known and familiar among data scientists. It is uses for 2D plotting for tailoring dynamic figures in multiple formats around the structures respectively.

10. TensorFlow: through the use of empowered ML algorithms, it is used for computing the data low graphs mainly. The more importantly, the library was tailored to accomplish the neural network work. High demands for training

11. Seaborn: This was tailored for the purpose visualizing complex statistical models. It comes with the ability and capability to deliver accurate graphs such as heat maps. Seaborn is created using the idea of the Matplotlib. Due to this, it is highly reliant on the Matplotli.

12. Bokeh: It is created for the purpose of interactive plots. This is one of the various visual purpose libraries. In conjunction with Seaborn, sit is also designed using the Matplotlib concept.

13. Plotly: this is one of the vast used and well known web based structure. This framework uses a various varieties of API supported by the multiple

programming languages such as Python, to offer visualization models of design.

14. NLTK: This is the short form for Natural Language Toolkit. Initially, it was designed to support teaching models used in AI and linguistic models: This is alongside NLP enabled research such as the cognitive theory. It enables achieving of natural language processing tasks.

15. Gensim: Through the use of implemented range of tools, this Python-based open source library allows topic modeling and space vector computation. It is compatible with the big test and creates a well-organized t operation and in-memory processing.

16. Scrapy: This python library is accountable for retrieving structured data out of web applications and for crawling on the programs. Similarly, known as spider bots, scrapy is a Python written open source library created for scraping.

17. Statsmodels: this is another Python library, accountable for giving exploration modules. Statsmodels mainly uses multiple methods for carrying out statistical analysis and assertions.

18. Kivy: The open source library licensed under MIT. It is highly useful in the creation of mobile apps accompanied by multi-touch applications. This Python library is accountable for supplying of a natural user interface that can effectively be accessed through Linux, Android and even windows.

19. PyQt: This is a free application which is licensed under the General Public License (GNU). It is having executed as the Python plugin. The Python connecting toolkit is being used as a cross-platform GUI.

20. OpenCV: This open source Intel created platform is licensed with BSD. It is tailored for driving the growth of real-time computation application development.

Python Crash Course

One of the best coding languages that you are able to work with when you want to start handling your own data science project is the Python language. This is a fantastic language that is able to take on all of the work that you want to do with data science and has the power that is needed to help create some great machine learning algorithms. With that said, it is still a great option for beginners because it has been designed to work with those who have never done programming before. While you can choose to work with the R programming language as well, you will find that the Python language is one of the best options because of its ease of use and power that combines together.

The Statements

The first thing that we are going to take a moment to look through when it comes to our Python language is the keywords. This is going to focus on the lines or sentences that you would like to have the compiler show up on your screen. You will need to use some of the keywords that we will talk about soon, and then you can tell the compiler what statements to put up on the screen. If you would like to leave a message on the screen such as what we can do with the Hello, World! The program, you will need to use that as your statement, and the print keyword, so the complier knows how to behave.

The Python Operators

We can also take some time to look at what is known as the Python operators. These are often going to get ignored when it comes time to write out codes because they don't seem like they are that important. But if you skip out on writing them, they are going to really make it so that your code will not work the way that you would like. There are a number of different types of Python operators that we are able to focus on, so making sure that you know what each kind is all about, and when to add these into your code, will make a world of difference as well.

The Keywords

The keywords are another important part of our Python code that we need to take a look at. These are going to be the words that we need to reserve because they are responsible for giving the compiler the instructions or the commands that you would like for it to use. These key words ensure that the code is going to perform the way that you would like it to the whole time.

These keywords need to be reserved, so make sure that you are not using them in the wrong places. If you do not use these keywords in the right manner, or you don't put them in the right place, then the compiler is going to end up with some issues understanding what you would like it to do, and you will not be able to get the results that you want. Make sure to learn the important keywords that come with the Python language and learn how to put them in the right spot of your code to get the best results with it.

Working with Comments

As we work with the Python coding, there are going to be times when we need to spend our time working with something that is known as a comment. This is going to be one of the best things that we are able to do in order to make sure that we can name a part of the code, or when we want to leave a little note for yourself or for another programmer, then you are going to need to work with some of the comments as well.

These comments are going to be a great option to work with. They are going to allow you to really leave a nice message in the code, and the compiler will know that it should just skip over that part of the code, and not read through it at all. It is as simple as that and can save you a lot of hassle and work inside of any code you are doing.

So, any time that you would like to write out a comment inside of your Python code, you just need to use the # symbol, and then the compiler will know that it is supposed to skip over that part of the code and not read it. We are able to add in as many of these comments as we would like into the code. Just remember to keep these to the number that is necessary, rather than going overboard with this, because it ensures that we are going to keep the code looking as nice and clean as possible.

The Python Class

You can store anything that you want inside a class that you design, but you must ensure that things that are similar end up in the same class. The items don't have to be identical to each other, but when someone takes a look at the class that you worked on, they need to be able to see that those objects belong together and make sense to be together.

For example, you don't have to just put cars into the same class, but you could have different vehicles in the same class. You could have items that are considered food. You can even have items that are all the same color. You get some freedom when creating the classes and storing objects in those classes, but when another programmer looks at the code, they should be able to figure out what the objects inside that class are about and those objects should share something in common.

Classes are very important when it comes to writing out your code. These are going to hold onto the various objects that you write in the code and can ensure that everything is stored properly. They will also make it easier for you to call out the different parts of your code when you need them for execution.

How to Name Your Identifiers

Inside the Python language, there are going to be a number of identifiers that we need to spend some time on. Each of these identifiers is going to be important, and they are going to make a big difference in some of the different parts of the code that you are able to work with. They are going to come to us under a lot of different names, but you will find that they are going to follow the same kinds of rules when it comes to naming them, and that can make it a lot easier for a beginner to work with as well.

To start with, you can use a lot of different types of characters in order to handle the naming of the identifiers that you would like to work with. You are able to use any letter of the alphabet that you would like, including uppercase and lowercase, and any combination of the two that you would like. Using numbers and the underscore symbol is just fine in this process as well.

With this in mind, there are going to be a few rules that you have to remember when it comes to naming your identifiers. For example, you are not able to start out a name with the underscore symbol or with a number. So, writing something like 3puppies or _threepuppies would not work. But you can do it with something like threepuppies for the name. A programmer also won't be able to add in spaces between the names either. You can write out threepuppies or three_puppies if you would like, but do not add the space between the two of them.

In addition to some of these rules, we need to spend some time looking at one other rule that is important to remember. Pick out a name for your identifier that is easy to remember and makes sense for that part of the code. This is going to ensure that you are able to understand the name and that you will be able to remember it later on when you need to call it up again.

Python Functions

Another topic that we are going to take a quick look at here as we work with the Python language is the idea of the Python functions. These are going to be a set of expressions that can also be statements inside of your code as well. You can have the choice to give them a name or let them remain anonymous. They are often the first-class objects that we are able to explore as well, meaning that your restrictions on how to work with them will be lower than we will find with other class objects.

Now, these functions are very diversified and there are many attributes that you can use when you try to create and bring up those functions. Some of the choices that you have with these functions include:

__doc__: This is going to return the docstring of the function that you are requesting.

Func_default: This one is going to return a tuple of the values of your default argument.

Func_globals: This one will return a reference that points to the dictionary holding the global variables for that function.

Func_dict: This one is responsible for returning the namespace that will support the attributes for all your arbitrary functions.

Func_closure: This will return to you a tuple of all the cells that hold the bindings for the free variables inside of the function.

There are different things that you can do with your functions, such as passing it as an argument over to one of your other functions if you need it. Any function that is able to take on a new one as the argument will be considered the higher-order function in the code. These are good to learn because they are important to your code as you move.

The Importance of Variables

While we are working with the Python programming language, we are going to run across sometimes when we need to work with the Python variables. These are going to be spaces in the memory of our computer that are able to hold spaces for the different values that are in any code that we are writing. This makes it easier for the code to pull up what is needed at the right times, simply by calling up the variable that we ask for as well.

Assigning a value to a variable is a pretty easy process. We just need to name the variable and then use the equal sign in order to get it all done. As long as the equal sign is in between the two, your compiler is going to know which value is going to be assigned back to which variable that is in the system. And if you would like to assign more than one value to a single variable, you would just need to make sure that there is an equal sign that falls in between all of that as well.

As we can see with some of the different parts that we have just looked through in this guidebook, learning how to work with the Python coding language is a great option to work with as well. Even if you have never spent any time working with coding in the past, and you are looking to just get into it in order to learn how to work with data science and one of these projects for your company.

Data Munging

The Process

Data munging comes after uploading the data, however at the moment that raw data cannot be used for any kind of analysis. Data can be chaotic, and filled with senseless information or gaps. This is why, as an aspiring data scientist, you solve this problem with the use of Python data structures that will turn this data into a data set that contains variables. You will need these data sets when working with any kind of statistical or machine learning analysis. Data munging might not be the most exciting phase in data science, but it is the foundation for your project and much needed to extract the valuable data you seek to obtain.

In the next phase, once you observe the data you obtain, you will begin to create a hypothesis that will require testing. You will examine variables graphically, and come up with new variables. You will use various data science methodologies such as machine learning or graph analysis in order to establish the most effective variables and their parameters. In other words, in this phase you process all the data you obtain from the previous phase and you create a model from it. You will undoubtedly realize in your testing that corrections are needed and you will return to the data munging phase to try something else. It's important to keep in mind that most of the time, the solution for your hypothesis will be nothing like the actual solution you will have at the end of a successful project. This is why you cannot work purely theoretically. A good data scientist is required to prototype a large variety of potential solutions and put them all to the test until the best course of action is revealed.

One of the most essential parts of the data science process is visualizing the results through tables, charts, and plots. In data science, this is referred to as "OSEMN", which stands for "Obtain, Scrub, Explore, Model, Interpret". While this abbreviation doesn't entirely illustrate the process behind data science, it captures the most important stages you should be aware of as an aspiring data scientist. Just keep in mind that data munging will often take the majority of your efforts when working on a project.

Importing Datasets with pandas

We need pandas to first start by loading the tabular data, such as spreadsheets and databases, from any files. This tool is great because it will create a data structure where every row will be indexed, variables kept separate by delimiters, data can be converted, and more.

You can explore the object's content just to see how it looks for now by typing the following line:

In: iris.head()

As you can see, we aren't using any parameters with these commands, so what you should get is a table with only the first 5 rows, because that's the default if there are no arguments. However, if you want a certain number of rows to be displayed, simply type the instruction like this:

iris.head(3)

Now you should see the first three rows instead. Next, let's access the column names by typing:

In: iris.columns

Out: Index(['sepal_length', 'sepal_width', 'petal_length',

'petal_width', 'target'], dtype='object')

The result of this will be a pandas index of the column names that looks like a list. Let's extract the target column. You can do it like this:

In: Y = iris['target']

Y

Out:

0Iris-setosa

1Iris -setosa

2Iris -setosa

3Iris -setosa

...

149Iris-virginica

Name: target, dtype: object

For now it's important only to understand that Y is a pandas series. That means it is similar to an array, but in this case it's one directional. Another thing that we notice in this example is that the pandas Index class is just like a dictionary index. Now let's type the following:

In: X = iris[['sepal_length', 'sepal_width']]

All we did now was asking for a list of columns by index. By doing so, we received a pandas dataframe as the result. In the first example, we received a one dimensional pandas series. Now we have a matrix instead, because we requested multiple columns. What's a matrix? If your basic math is a bit rusty, you should know that it is an array of numbers that are arranged in rows and columns.

Next, we want to have the dimensions of the dataset:

In: print (X.shape)

Out: (150, 2)

In: print (Y.shape)

Out: (150,)

What we have now is a tuple. We can now see the size of the array in both dimensions. Now that you know the basics of this process, let's move on to basic preprocessing.

Preprocessing Data with pandas

The next step after learning how to load datasets is to get accustomed to the data preprocessing routines. Let's say we want to apply a function to a certain section of rows. To achieve this, we need a mask. What's a mask? It's a series of true or false values (Boolean) that we need to tell when a certain line is selected. As always, let's examine an example because reading theory can be dry and confusing.

In: mask_feature = iris['sepal_length'] > 6.0

In: mask_feature

0False

1False

...

146True

147True

148True

149False

In this example we're trying to select all the lines of our "iris" dataset that have the value of "sepal length" larger than 6. You can clearly see the observations that are either true or false, and therefore know the ones that fit our query. Now let's use a mask in order to change our "iris-virginica" target with a new label. Type:

In: mask_target = iris['target'] == 'Iris-virginica'

In: iris.loc[mask_target, 'target'] = 'New label'

All "Iris-virginica" labels will now be shown as "New label" instead. We are using the "loc()" method to access this data with row and column indexes. Next, let's take a look at the new label list in the "target" column. Type:

In: iris['target'].unique()

Out: array(['Iris-setosa', 'Iris-versicolor', 'New label'], dtype=object)

In this example we are using the "unique" method to examine the new list. Next we can check the statistics by grouping every column. Let's see this in action first, and then discuss how it works. Type:

In: grouped_targets_mean = iris.groupby(['target']).mean()

grouped_targets_mean

Out:

```
In: grouped_targets_var = iris.groupby(['target']).var()
grouped_targets_var
Out:
```

We start by grouping each column with the "groupby" method. If you are a bit familiar with SQL, it's worth noting that this works similarly to the "GROUP BY" instruction. Next, we use the "mean" method, which computes the average of the values. This is an aggregate method that can be applied to one or several columns. Then we can have several other pandas methods such as "var" which stands for the variance, "sum" for the summation, "count" for the number of rows, and more. Keep in mind that the result you are looking at is still a data frame. That means that you can link as many operations as you want. In our example we are using the "groupby" method to group the observations by label and then check what the difference is between the values and variances for each of our groups.

Now let's assume the dataset contains a time series. What's a time series, you ask? In data science, sometimes we have to analyze a series of data points that are graphed in a certain chronological order. In other words, it is a sequence of the equally spaced points in time. Time series are used often in statistics, for weather forecasting, and for counting sunspots. Often, these datasets have really noisy data points, so we have to use a "rolling" operation, like this:

```
In: smooth_time_series = pd.rolling_mean(time_series, 5)
```

Now let's explore pandas "apply" method that has many uses due to its ability to perform programmatically operations on rows and columns. Let's see this in action by counting the number of non-zero elements that exist in each line.

In: iris.apply(np.count_nonzero, axis=1).head()

Out:05

15

25

35

45

dtype: int64

Lastly, let's use the "applymap" method for element level operations. In the next example, we are going to assume we want the length of the string representation of each cell. Type:

In: iris.applymap(lambda el:len(str(el))).head()

To receive our value, we need to cast every individual cell to a string value. Once that is done, we can gain the value of the length.

Data Selection with pandas

The final section about working with pandas is data selection. Let's say you find yourself in a situation where your dataset has an index column, and you need to import it and then manipulate it. To visualize this, let's say we have a dataset with an index from 100. Here's how it would look:

n,val1,val2,val3

100,10,10,C

101,10,20,C

102,10,30,B

103,10,40,B

104,10,50,A

So the index of row 0 is 100. If you import such a file, you will have an index column like in our case labeled as "n". There's nothing really wrong with it, however you might use the index column by mistake, so you should separate it instead in order to prevent such errors from happening. To avoid possible issues and errors, all you need to do is mention that "n" is an index column. Here's how to do it:

In: dataset = pd.read_csv('a_selection_example_1.csv',

index_col=0) dataset

Out:

Your index column should now be separate. Now let's access the value inside any cell. There's more than one way to do that. You can simply target it by mentioning the column and line. Let's assume we want to obtain "Val3" from the 5th line, which is marked by an index of 104.

In: dataset['val3'][104]

Out: 'A'

Keep in mind that this isn't a matrix, even though it might look like one. Make sure to specify the column first, and then the row in order to extract the value from the cell you want.

Categorical and Numerical Data

Numerical data is quite self-explanatory, as it deals with any data expressed in numbers, such as temperature or sums of money.

Categorical data, on the other hand, is expressed by a value that can't be measured. A great example of this type of data, which is sometimes referred to as nominal data, is the weather, which holds values such as sunny, partially cloudy, and so on. Basically, data to which you cannot apply equal to, greater than, or less than operators is nominal data. Other examples of this data include products you purchase from an online store, computer IDs, IP addresses, etc. Booleans are the one thing that is needed to work with both categorical and numerical data. They can even be used to encode categorical values as numerical values. Let's see an example:

Categorical_feature = sunnynumerical_features = [1, 0, 0, 0, 0]

Categorical_feature = foggynumerical _features = [0, 1, 0, 0, 0]

Categorical_feature = snowynumerical _features = [0, 0, 1, 0, 0]

Categorical_feature = rainynumerical _features = [0, 0, 0, 1, 0]

Categorical_feature = cloudynumerical _features = [0, 0, 0, 0, 1]

This turns the information into a map with 5 true or false statements for each categorical feature we listed. One of the numerical features (1) confirms the categorical feature, while the other four are o. Now let's turn this result into a dataframe that presents each categorical feature as a column and the numerical features next to that column. To achieve this you need to type the following code:

In: import pandas as pd

categorical_feature = pd.Series(['sunny', 'foggy', 'snowy', 'rainy', 'cloudy'])

mapping = pd.get_dummies(categorical_feature)

mapping

Out:

In data science, this is called binarization. We do not use one categorical feature with as many levels as we have. Instead, we create all the categorical features and assign two binary values to them. Next we can map the categorical values to a list of numerical values. This is how it would look:

In: mapping['sunny']

Out:

01.0

10.0

20.0

30.0

40.0

Name: sunny, dtype: float64

In: mapping['foggy']

Out:

00.0

11.0

```
20.0

30.0

40.0

Name: cloudy, dtype: float64
```

Why Data Preprocessing Is Important

What Is Data Preprcoessing?

Let's suppose that you are going through some of the log files of a website and analyzing these, hoping to find out which IP out of all the options the spammers are coming from.

Or you can use this to figure out which demographic on the website is leading to more sales.

An analysis has to be performed on the data with two important columns to provide answers to such questions and more.

These are going to include the number of hits that have been made to the website, and the IP address of the hit.

As we can imagine here, the log files that you are analyzing are not going to be structured, and they could contain a lot of textual information that is unstructured.

To keep this simple, preparing the log file to extract the data in the format that you require in order to analyze it can be the process known as data preparation.

Data preparation is a big part of the whole data science process.

According to CrowdFlower, which is a provider of data enrichment platforms that data scientists can work with, it is seen that out of 80 data scientists, they will spend their day in the following:

60 percent of their time is spent on organizing and then cleaning the data they have collected.

19 percent is spent on collecting the sets of data that they want to use.

9 percent is used to mine the data that they have collected and prepared in order to draw the necessary patterns.

3 percent of their time will be spent doing any of the necessary training for the sets of data.

4 percent of the time is going to be spent trying to refine the algorithms that were created and working on getting them better at their jobs.

5 percent of the time is spent on some of the other tasks that are needed for this job.

As we can see from the statistics of the survey above, it helps us to see that most of the time for that data scientist is spent in preparing the data, which means they have to spend a good deal of time organizing, cleaning, and collecting, before they are even able to start on the process of analyzing the data.

The amount of time that you actually will spend on preparing the data for a specific problem with the analysis is going to depend directly on the health of the data.

If there are a lot of errors, missing parts, and duplicate values, then this is a process that will take a lot longer.

Why Do I Need Data Preprocessing?

One question that a lot of people have when it is time to work on the process of data preparation is why they need to do it in the first place.

It may seem to someone who is just getting started in this field that collecting the data and getting it all as organized as possible would be the best steps to take, and then they can go on to making their own model.

But there are a few different reasons why data preparation will be so important to this process, and they will include the following:

The set of data that you are working with could contain a few discrepancies in the codes or the names that you are using.

The set of data that you are working with could contain a lot of outliers or some errors that mess with the results.

The set of data that you are working with will lack your attributes of interest to help with the analysis.

The set of data that you want to explore is not going to be qualitative, but it is going to be quantitative.

These are not the same things, and often having more quality is going to be the most important.

Each of these things has the potential to really mess up the model that you are working on and could get you results or predictions that are not as accurate as you would like.

Taking the time to prepare your data and get it clean and ready to go can solve this issue and will ensure that your data is going to be more than ready to use in no time.

What Are the Steps for Data Preprocessing?

At this point, we need to take some time to look at some of the steps that are needed to handle the data preparation for data mining.

The first step is to clean the data.

This is one of the first and most important steps to handling the data and getting it prepared.

We need to go through and correct any of the data that is inconsistent by filling out some of the values that are missing and then smoothing out the outliers and any data that is making a lot of noise and influencing the analysis in a negative manner.

There is the possibility that we end up with many rows in our set of data that do not have a value for the attributes of interest, or they could be inconsistent data that is there as well.

In some cases, there are records that have been duplicated or some other random error that shows up.

We need to tackle all of these issues with the data quality as quickly as possible in order to get a model at the end that provides us with an honest and reliable prediction.

There are a few methods that we can use to handle some of the missing values.

The method that is chosen is going to be dependent on the requirement either by ignoring the tuple or filling in some of the missing values with the mean value of the attribute.

This can be done with the help of the global constant or with some of the other Python machine learning techniques, including the Bayesian formulae or a decision tree.

We can also take some time to tackle the noisy data when needed.

It is possible to handle this in a manual manner.

Or there are several techniques of clustering or regression that can help us to handle this as well. You have to choose the one that is needed based on the data that you have.

The second step that we need to focus on here is going to be known as data integration.

This step is going to involve a few things like integrating the schema, resolving some of the conflicts of the data if any shows up, and even handling any of the redundancies that show up in the data that you are using.

Next on the list is going to be the idea of data transformation.

This step is going to be important because it will take the time to handle some of the noise that is found in your data.

This step is going to help us to take out that noise from the data so it will not cause the analysis you have to go wrong.

We can also see the steps of normalization, aggregation, and generalization showing up in this step as well.

We can then move on to the fourth step, which is going to be all about reducing the data.

a reduced representation of their set of data.

We want this set to be smaller in size than some of the others, but inclusive enough that it will provide us with some of the same analysis outcomes that we want.

This can be hard when we have a very large set of data, but there are a few reduction strategies for the data that we can apply.

Some of these are going to include the numerosity reduction, aggregation, data cube, and dimensionality reduction, and more, based on the requirements that you have.

And finally, the fifth step of this is going to be known as data discretization.

The set of data that you are working with will contain three types of attributes.

Some of the algorithms that you will choose to work with only handle the attributes that are categorical.

This step of data discretization can help someone in data science divide continuous attributes into intervals, and can also help reduce the size of the data.

This helps us to prepare it for analysis.

Take your time with this one to make sure that it all matches up and does some of the things that you are expecting.

Many of the methods and the techniques that you are able to use with this part of the process are going to be strong and can get a lot of the work with you.

But even with all of these tools, it is still considered an area of research, one that many scientists are going to explore more and hopefully come up with some new strategies and techniques that you can use to get it done.

Handling the Missing Data

It is common for data to become missing in many applications of data analysis.

One of the goals of working with the Pandas library here is that we want to make working with some of this missing data as easy and as painless as possible.

For example, all of the descriptive statistics that happen on the objects of Pandas exclude the missing data by default.

The way that this data is going to be represented in Pandas is going to have some problems, but it can be really useful for many of the users who decide to go with this kind of library.

For some of the numeric data that we may have to work with, the Pandas library is going to work with a floating-point value that is known as NaN, or not a number, to represent the data that is missing inside of our set of data.

In the Pandas library, we have adopted a convention that is used in the programming language of R in order to refer to the missing data.

This missing data is going to show up as NA, which means not available right now.

In the applications of statistics, NA data can either be data that doesn't exist at all, or that exists, but we are not going to be able to observe through problems with collecting the data.

When cleaning up the data to be analyzed, it is often important to do some of the analysis on the missing data itself to help identify the collection of the data and any problems or potential biases in the data that has been caused by the missing data.

There are also times when the data is going to have duplicates.

When you get information online or from other sets of data, it is possible that some of the results will be duplicated.

If this happens often, then there is going to be a mess with the insights and predictions that you get.

The data is going to lean towards the duplicates, and it will not work the way that you would like.

There are ways that you can work with the Pandas library in order to really improve this and make sure that the duplicates are eliminated or are at least limited at least a little bit.

There is so much that we are able to do when it comes to working with data preparation in order to complete the process of data mining and getting the results that we want in no time with our analysis.

Make sure to take some time on this part, as it can really make or break the system that we are trying to create.

If you do spend enough time on it, and ensure that the data is as organized and clean as possible, you are going to be happy with the results and ready to take on the rest of the process.

What is Data Wrangling?

During the import, you have to map the data headers in your export file to the values the email service recognizes. You have to set the rule of declaring "email ID" is the same as "email address" to avoid any data errors. After the import is complete, the customer details are saved in the email service database. This is a simple example of data wrangling. Here are some tools used for data wrangling:

The NumPy and SciPy Library

The first two libraries that we are going to explore here are going to be the NumPy, or Numeric and Scientific Computation, and the SciPy library. NumPy is a useful library to learn about because it is going to help us lay down some of the basic premises that are needed for any kind of scientific computing that we wish to do with Python. It is also going to be there to help us grab the functions that we need, many of which are precompiled and fast enough to help out with any and all mathematical and numerical routines.

In addition to some of the listed benefits that we have above, NumPy is also able to help us optimize some of the programming that we want to do with Python. The way that it can do this is to add in a few powerful data structures along the way. what this does is makes it easier for us to efficiently compute the arrays and the matrices that we have, especially when one or both of these are considered multi-dimensional.

Then we have SciPy, or Scientific Python, which is going to come with NumPy in many cases. Often you can't get one to work well without the other because they share many features. When you are working with SciPy, you are able to gain that competitive edge even more than just using NumPy on its own. This happens when you try to enhance some of the useful functions for regression, minimization, and so much more.

The Pandas Library

The next library that we need to spend some time on when we are looking for help with one of our data analytics projects is going to be known as Pandas, or the Python Data Analysis Library. You will find that the name gives away why this library is so important, and why we need to spend some time working with this as well.

Pandas are going to be one of the tools that work with Python, and it is also open-sourced so you can download it and start working with it without any problems. It is going to provide us with some great and easy data structures to work with, and it has a lot of high-performance abilities that will help as well. In fact, you will find that the Pandas library is able to help us out with all of the different programming things that we want to do when it comes to finishing the data analysis.

You are able to work with this library in particular when you want to add in some new structures of data and some new tools to help with the data analysis. And you will find that this work regardless of the kind of project that you would like to complete. There are many industries and companies that are fond of working with this kind of library to help them with things like finance, social science, engineering, and statistics to name a few.

The best part about using this library is that it is adaptable, which helps us to get more work done. It also works with any kind of data that you were able to collect for it, including uncategorized, messy, unstructured, and incomplete data. Even once you have the data, this library is going to step in and help provide us with all of the tools that we need to slice, reshape, merge, and more all of the sets of data we have.

Pandas are going to come with a variety of features that makes it perfect for data science. Some of the best features that come with the Pandas library from Python will include:

The Matplotlib Library

When you are working with some of the visuals that are needed in data analysis, you will find that the matplotlib library is one of the best ones that you would like to work with. This helps you to really visualize and understand all of the information that you have collected and really helps you to figure out the relationships that are going to come up with your models. It is also going to make it more efficient to see how the insights are going to be worth your time.

Working with these visuals is going to be so important. Depending on the kind of data that is in your models and that you have been working with the whole time, you will find that these visuals are going to make it easier to see what information you have gathered, and how the different parts are going to work when you try to combine them together.

This is one of the areas where you will see that this library is going to be useful. It is basically going to be a 2D plotting library that you are able to use with Python, and it can really help us by producing figures that are publication quality in a lot of formats. You will also see that it can offer you a variety of interactive environments to work with that can handle many platforms based on your needs. This library can be used with scripts from Python, Jupyter, IPython, and more to help get things done.

This library is able to help with generating scatterplots, error charts, bar charts, power spectra, histograms, and plots to name a few. If you need to have some kind of chart or graph to go along with your data analysis, make sure to check out what the matplotlib option can do for you.

The Scikit-Learn Library

While we are on the topic, we need to spend a few minutes looking at the Scikit-Learn library and how well it is able to handle some of the machine learning and data analysis work that you want to do with Python. This one is going to have a ton of algorithms that work well with machine learning and these algorithms can often fit under the idea of supervised and unsupervised machine learning problems that are low to medium scale. This means that there are a lot of potential uses and applications to make all of this work.

When you are working with the Python language, and working with the Scikit-Learn library to help out with some of the machine learning, you will find that the main emphasis that we are going to see will be on things like how easy it is to use, the performance of the model, a bit on the documentation, and the consistency that we are able to get to show up on the API.

The TensorFlow Library

We can also work with the library that is known as TensorFlow. This is actually considered one of the best libraries out there that works with Python and can handle the work that you want to do with data science. This is a library that was originally released by the Google Brain Team. It was written out mostly with the help of the C++ language, which is a bit different but it comes with some of the bindings in Python, so you will be able to still use the language that you have been learning without having to worry about it.

One of the best features that you will see with the TensorFlow library is that it is going to have a flexible architecture that is nice for allowing the programmer to deploy it with one or more GPU's or CPUs on your device whether that is a server, a mobile, or a desktop device. And you can do all of this with the same API the whole time.

The Keras Library

Keras is going to be an open-sourced library form Python that is able to help you to build up your own neural networks, at a high level of the interface. It is going to be pretty minimalistic, which makes it easier to work with, and the coding on this library is going to be simple and straightforward, while still adding in some of the high-level extensibility that you need. It is going to work either TensorFlow or Theano along with CNTK as the backend to make this work better. We can remember that the API that comes with Keras is designed for humans to use, rather than humans, which makes it easier to use and puts the experience of the user right in front.

Keras is going to work with all of the best-known practices at the time when it is necessary to reduce the cognitive load. This Python library is going to offer us a consistent and simple API that will help us to minimize how many actions that the user has to do for the different parts of the code that are common, and it also helps to provide feedback that is actionable and clear if you do end up with an error on the code.

The Theano Library

Theano is another great library to work with during data science, and it is often seen as one of the highly-rated libraries to get this work done. In this library, you will get the benefit of defining, optimizing, and then evaluating many different types of mathematical expressions that come with multi-dimensional arrays in an efficient manner. This library is able to use lots of GPUs and perform symbolic differentiation in a more efficient manner.

Theano is a great library to learn how to use, but it does come with a learning curve that is pretty steep, especially for most of the people who have learned how to work with Python because declaring the variables and building up some of the functions that you want to work with will be quite a bit different from the premises that you learn in Python.

However, this doesn't mean that the process is impossible. It just means that you need to take a bit longer to learn how to make this happen. With some good tutorials and examples, it is possible for someone who is brand new to Theano to get this coding all done. Many great libraries that come with Python, including Padas and NumPy, will be able to make this a bit easier as well.

Inheritances to Clean Up the Code

In the general sense of things, inheritance is a tool that allows users to define a class, which derives all its functionality from a parent class while providing insight to add more.

Inheritance forms a core part of object programming because of how it can extend the functionality of an already existing class by introducing new features. It can be compared to a real-world situation of a birthright in which children inherit the properties of their parents in addition to the ones they already possess. The children may also derive a surname (the last name) from their parents. The inheritance serves as one of the four core concepts object-oriented programming (OOP), including polymorphism, abstraction, and encapsulation. Inheritance is a robust tool in the hands of programmers, allowing them to create and enable new classes to inherit or receive every one of the methods and properties of an already existing class or classes. As we have come to know, class refers to a template or blueprint of an object. As such, every object was created using a class, while the concept of inheritance comes in to devise a form of relationship between the blueprints. This property is a feature of object-oriented programming that is applied in defining a new class containing little to no modification to an already existing class. While the class from which the other class is obtained is known as the parent class or base class, the created class is regarded as the child class or derived class. The formation of the derived class involves the use of the base class, as well as some other added features. The general purpose of the concept of inheritance is to help improve code reusability.

The function of inheritance in object-oriented programming:

By making use of the inheritance feature, users can find it possible to have a blueprint that has the same attributes as the initial one.

How an Inheritance is Implemented in Python

To introduce inheritance into a code sample, you could use the following syntax:

```
class ParentClass:
 Parent class attributes
 Parent class methods
class ChildClass(ParentClass):
 Child class attributes
 Child class methods
```

Automatically, inheritance introduces reusability to a block of code because the child class comprises of everything found in the base class.

Methods of interaction between a parent and child class

When programmers make use of a concept in object-oriented programming like inheritance, they create interactions between parent and child classes in three main ways. They include:

Anything performed on the child class modifies a corresponding action performed on the parent class.

Actions carried out on the child class override the subsequent actions carried out on the parent class.

Actions performed on the child class are simple actions performed on the parent class.

Sample code for Python inheritance

To improve your understanding of the concept of inheritance and its application, let us consider some samples below:

We start by creating a base or parent class, with a child or derived class vehicle.

```
class Taxi:

def___init__(self, model, capacity, variant):

self.__model = model     #___model is private to Taxi class

self.__capacity = capacity

self.__variant = variant

defgetModel(self):          # getmodel() is accessible outside the class

      return self.__model

defgetCapacity(self):          # getCapacity() function is accessible to class
Vehicle

      return self.__capacity

defsetCapacity(self, capacity): # setCapacity() is accessible outside the
class

self.__capacity = capacity
```

```
defgetVariant(self):        # getVariant() function is accessible to class
Vehicle
    return self.__variant
defsetVariant(self, variant): # setVariant() is accessible outside the class
self.__variant = variant
class Vehicle(Taxi):
def__init__(self, model, capacity, variant, color):
    # call parent constructor to set model and color
    super().__init__(model, capacity, variant)
self.__color = color
defvehicleInfo(self):
    return self.getModel() + " " + self.getVariant() + " in "+ self.__color
+ " with " + self.getCapacity() + " seats"
# In method getInfo we can call getmodel(), getCapacity() as they are
# accessible in the child class through inheritance
v1 = Vehicle("i20 Active", "4", "SX", "Bronze")
print(v1.vehicleInfo())
print(v1.getModel()) # Vehicle has no method getModel() but it is
accessible via Vehicle class
v2 = Vehicle("Fortuner", "7", "MT2755", "White")
print(v2.vehicleInfo())
```

print(v2.getModel()) # Vehicle has no method getModel() but it is accessible via Vehicle class

Take note that the getName() method used in the sample code for the vehicle class is unspecified. The reason is linked to the fact that the vehicle class receives it from its parent class.

So, when the sample code is executed, the result will be the following:

output

i20 Active SX in Bronze with 4 seats

i20 Active

Fortuner MT2755 in White with 7 seats

Fortuner

The UML Diagram of Python Inheritance

To provide more clarity on this subject, take a look at the UML diagram outlined below. The diagram is connected to the sample code used.

The Super() Method:

What is the function of the super() method in Python?

The super() method enables users to gain access to the inherited methods which cascade into a class object. In the samples shown earlier, the super() method was used within the constructor of the derived class <Vehicle>. At this point, the super() method invokes the function of the parent class <Taxi>.

How the super() method is implemented

Assume that you are required to involve a method in the parent class, for example, vehicleinfo(), that is defined in the derived class. To do this, you can make use of the line of code showed below:

```
super().vehicleInfo()
```

In the same vein, it is possible to income the parent class constructor from the sub or child class__init__making use of the command below:

```
super().__init__()
```

Implicit inheritance in Python:

Implicit actions happen in Python inheritance whenever a programmer defines a function within the base class alone. This type of inheritance is depicted in syntax using the simple sample shown below:

```
class super (object) :

def implicit(self) :

     print ("Super-Class with Implicit function")

class sub(super) :
```

```
  pass
su = super()
sb = sub()
su.implicit()
sb.implicit()
```

The output produced is as follows::

```
Super-Class with Implicit function
Super-Class with Implicit function
```

From a general overview, it can be seen that Python inheritance contributes immensely to object-oriented programming. As a result, it is of utter importance that you understand how inheritance works in Python owing to the object-oriented design of the language.

Reading and writing data

How to Read and Write Data in Text Format

Python is considered a powerful programming language for manipulating text files because of its simple syntax to interact directly with the files, features such as tuple packing/unpacking, and well-built data structures.

There are numerous functions present in pandas library to perform read operation on tabular data. Here is a table listing some of the functions.

Function name	Description of the function
read_csv	It is used to load the data from a file or a URL using a delimiter. It uses comma as the default delimiter.
read_table	It is used to load the data from a file or a URL usinga delimiter. It uses tab as the default delimiter.
read_fwf	It is used to read the data, which is present in a fixed width column format having no delimiters in it.
read_clipboard	It is a similar version of data_table. But it doesn't read the data from files and uses the clipboard data for reading purpose. Thus, it comes handy to convert tables present in webpages.

Let us see an overview about how to use the above functions for converting the text file's data into a DataFrame. Here are the options under which the above functions fall:

Date-time parsing: It covers the combining power to combine date and time data present in numerous columns into one sole column while showing the result.

Indexing: It has the capability to use one as well as more than one column while returning the DataFrame. It also has the option to choose or not to choose the column names present in the file.

Iteration: It has the capability to support iteration of a large amount of data present in the large size files.

Data conversion and type inference: It covers personalized list for the value markers, which are not present and conversions related to user defined values.

Skipping data: It includes row, footer, and numeric data skipping from the file.

The most important feature for any function is type inference. By using it, we you don't need to worry about describing the column type like integer, string, boolean, numeric, etc. Let us see one example of csv file (comma separated values).

Let's see an example:

In [154]: !cat chapter05/csvExample1.csv

w, x, y, z, word

10, 20, 30, 40, this

50, 60, 70, 80, is

90, 100, 110, 120, fun

As it is a csv file, we can use the comma as a delimiter and use read_csv function to read the file into a DataFrame.

In [155]: df = pd.read_csv('chapter05/csvExample1.csv')

In [156]: df

Out [156]:

wxyzword

0 10203040 this

1 50 60 70 80 is

2 90 100 110 120 fun

It can also be done using the read_table function by describing the delimiter.

In [157]: pd.read_table('chapter05/csvExample1.csv', sep=',')

Out [157]:

wxyzword

0 10203040 this

1 50 60 70 80 is

2 90 100 110 120 fun

Note: We have used the cat shell command for printing the contents present in the file. If you are using Unix, and instead using Windows, you need to use the keyword "type" and not "cat" to print it on your screen.

It's not necessary that every file will have a header row. Let's see the below example:

In [158]: !cat chapter05/csvExample2.csv

10, 20, 30, 40, this

50, 60, 70, 80, is

90, 100, 110, 120, fun

We have two options to read this. One is to permit the pandas library to automatically assign the default column names. The other option is to specify the column names on your own.

In [159]: pd.read_csv('chapter05/csvExample2.csv', header = None)

Out [159]:

X.1X.2X.3X.4X.5

0 10203040 this

1 50 60 70 80 is

2 90 100 110 120 fun

In [160]: pd.read_csv('chapter05/csvExample2.csv', names = ['w', 'x', 'y', 'z', 'word'])

Out [160]:

wxyzword

0 10203040 this

1 50 60 70 80 is

2 90 100 110 120 fun

If you want to arrange the values in a hierarchy using multiple columns, you can pass the list of column names or numbers. Here is an example:

In [161]: !cat chapter05/csvExample3.csv

firstKey, secondKey, firstValue, secondValue

one, w, 10, 20

one, x, 30, 40

one, y, 50, 60

one, z, 70, 80

two, w, 90, 100

two, x, 110, 120

two, y, 130, 140

two, z, 150, 160

In [162]: parse_data = pd.read_csv(' chapter05/csvExample3.csv', index_col=[' firstKey ', ' secondKey '])

In [163]: parse_data

Out [163]:

firstValuesecondValue

firstKey secondKey

onew 10 20

x 30 40

y 50 60

z 70 80

two w 90 100

x 110 120

y 130 140

z 150 160

Parser function provides a lot of additional arguments, which can be used to handle many file format exceptions. For example, skiprows allows you to skip any rows present in the text file. Let's see an example:

In [164]: !cat chapter05/csvExample4.csv

Hi!

We are making it a little bit difficult for you

w, x, y, z, word

In today's modern world, you can easily skip any rows present in a file

10, 20, 30, 40, this

50, 60, 70, 80, is

90, 100, 110, 120, fun

In [165]: pd.read_csv(' chapter05/csvExample4.csv', skiprows = [0, 1, 3])

Out [165]:

wxyzword

0 10203040 this

1 50 60 70 80 is

2 90 100 110 120 fun

A very important part in the parsing process, which is commonly used, is "Missing data handling". In these cases, either the missing data is not present in the file or it is marked as a sentinel value. In parsing, pandas use common sentinels like NA, NULL, and -1.

Now let us see an example:

In [166]: !cat chapter05/csvExample5.csv

anyValue , w, x, y, z, word

one, 10, 20, 30, 40, NA

NA, 50, 60 , , 80, is

three, NA, 100, 110, 120, fun

In [167]: final_result = pd.read_csv('chapter05/csvExample5.csv')

In [168]: final_result

Out [168]:

anyValue w x y z word

0 one 10 20 30 40 NaN

1 NaN 50 60 NaN 80 is

2 three NaN 100 110 120 fun

In [169]: pd.isnull(final_result)

Out [169]:

anyValue w x y z word

0 F alse Fal se Fa lse F alse F alse True

1 True False Fa lse True False F alse

2 False True False Fa lse F alse Fa lse

The option na_values will either take a set of string values or a list while considering the missing values in the text file.

In [170]: final_result = pd.read_csv(' chapter05/csvExample5.csv', na_values = ['NULL'])

In [171]: final_result

Out [171]:

anyValue w x y z word

0 one 10 20 30 40 NaN

1 NaN 50 60 NaN 80 is

2 three NaN 100 110 120 fun

We can specify fifferent NA sentinels for every column present in the text file.

Now let's see an example:

In [172]: sentinels = { 'word': ['fun', 'NA'], 'anyValue': ['one'] }

In [173]: pd.read_csv(chapter05/csvExample5.csv', na_values=sentinels)

Out [173]:

something a b c d message

anyValue w x y z word

0 NaN 10 20 30 40 NaN

1 NaN 50 60 NaN 80 is

2 three NaN 100 110 120 NaN

Argument name	Description of the argument
Path	It is a string value that is used to indicate the location of file, file-like objects, or the URL.
Delimiter or sep	It is used to split the columns present in each row by either using a regular expression or a character sequence.
Names	It is used to show the result in form of column names, combined with the header value as None.
na_values	It is used to provide the sequence of values, which needs to be replaced by NA
Header	It is used to provide the row number that will be used as column names. The default value is 0 and is None in case there is no header row present in the file.

comment	It is used to split the character(s) comments after the end of lines.
date_parser	It is used for parsing dates from a text file.
index_col	It is used to provide the column names or numbers that need to be used as row index in result.
Nrows	It I used to pass the number of rows, which need to be read from the starting point of the file.
Verbose	It is used to print different output information, such as total number of missing values that are present in non-numeric columns.
Iterator	It is used to return the TextParser object to read the file in steps.
convertors	It is used to perform name mapping on functions.
skip_footer	It is used to provide the number of lines, which needs to be ignored at the end of the file.
Squeeze	It is used to return a series if the parsed data has only one column present in it.
chunksize	It is used to iterate and provide size of the file chunks.
encoding	It is used to provide the text encoding for Unicode system.
Dayfirst	It is used to deal with international format when ambiguous dates are getting parsed. Its default value is false.

How to Read Small Pieces of Text Files

We will have to read the file in small pieces of rows instead of reading the complete file. It can be done using "nrows".

In [176]: pd.read_csv('chapter05/example6.csv', nrows = 10)

Out [176]:

wxyzword

0 10203040 A

1 50 60 70 80 B

2 90 100 110 120 C

3130140150160D

4170180190200E

510203040F

650607080G

790100110120H

8130140150160I

9170180190200J

In order to read the file, we can also use chunksize for number of rows.

In [177]: file_chunker = pd.read_csv('chapter05/example6.csv', chunksize = 500)

In [178]: file_chunker

Out [178]: <pandas.io.parsers.TextParser at 0x8398150>

TextParser object gets returned from read_csv will be iterating the file as per the chunksize fixed above i.e. 500. Therefore, we can aggregate the total value counts in "key" column by iterating the example6 file.

file_chunker = pd.read_csv('chapter05/example6.csv', chunksize = 500)

total = Series([])

for data_piece in file_chunker:

total = total.add(data_piece['key'].value_counts(), fill_value = 0)

total = total.order(ascending = False)

Now we will get the below result:

In [179]: total[:10]

Out [179]:

F 460

Y 452

J 445

P 438

R 429

N 417

K 407

V 400

B 391

D 387

TextParser also has a get_chunk method. It helps us to read the pieces of random size from the file.

The Different Types of Data We Can Work With

The information that is processed in computer programs is represented in various ways. If you treat numerical information, you will use simple or real values or simple data. If you work logical expressions with true or false results you will use logical or Boolean data. If, on the other hand, you manipulate text you will use data of type character or string of characters (string). To represent numerical information (or even logical or text) where the data is grouped in the form of tables, such as vectors and matrices, or more complex structures, composite data types will be used.

The types of data used in the main programming languages are shown in the figure below.

Note: The character data type does not exist in Python, a simple character is represented as a character string (string).

Structures composed of languages such as C, FORTRAN, Pascal, Matlab, etc. Py: Composite structures in Python. Source: self-made.

Simple data

The elementary data is simple, also called scalars because they are indivisible objects. Simple data are characterized by having a single value associated and are of the integer, real or floating-point (float), Boolean and character type. In Python, there is no simple character data type.

Although the data consists of only one letter or ASCII character it is represented as a data composed of a string of characters (string).

Integers

In mathematics, the integers are the natural numbers, their negatives and zero. Examples of integers: 5, -20, 0, -104. Numbers with decimal parts are not included among the integers, such as 3.4. Integers, in most programming languages including Python, are defined with the word int. Python has an internal type function that returns the given data type:

In C ++ or Pascal 4 bytes (32 bits are used, and one bit is reserved for the sign, signed 32-bit) for standard integers (int, integer), represented in the number range:

–2147483648… 2147483647

For greater range in these languages, 8 bytes (signed 64-bit) are used, declaring them as long or int64:

–263…….263 –1

Unlike C++ or Pascal, in Python integer data is stored with "arbitrary precision", that is, the number of bytes needed to represent the integer is used. For example, the numbers 5 (binary: 101) and 200 (27 + 26 + 23, binary: 11001000) are represented:

The internal Python bin (N) function converts an integer to string with the equivalent binary (0b + binary). To check the wide range of values in Python, let's test a value greater than 263, such as 2220

```
>>> 2**220
```

```
168499666669691498716668844293872691710232152640878578006
8975640576
```

Real

Unlike integers that are discrete values from one natural number to another, the continuous value numbers of the set of real numbers in Mathematics are called real or floating-point/point8, or simply float. Not all real numbers can be accurately represented in computer science because many have infinite decimal places. However, according to the level of precision, we want these numbers can be approximated well enough. The use of the IEEE 754 standard to represent real or floating-point numbers has been agreed for several decades, using scientific notation.

This notation allows you to represent numbers with a mantissa (significant digits) and an exponent separated by the letter 'e' or 'E'. For example, the number 4000 is represented by the mantissa 4 and the exponent 3, 4e3. It reads 4 times from 10 to 3. The number 0.25 is also represented as 25e-2. It is also allowed to omit the initial zero, .25 and the real number 4.0 can be entered as 4. (without the zero after the period).

Sign	Exponent	Mantista
1 Bit	11 Bits	52 Bits

Value= (-1)sign * 1.Mantisa * 2(Exponent-1023)

Thus, with 64 bits the numbers (decimals) of ± 5.0 * 10-324 (precision) can be represented up to ± 1.7 * 10308 range. The IEEE 754 standard updated in 2008 incorporates the decimal64 format that uses the decimal base to improve binary representation errors. Python incorporates the Decimal function of the decimal module.

Below are several examples of real numbers, the real type (float) and a typical error with representation of floating point with binary base, in the case of the value 0.1.

```
>>> 25e-2

0.25

>>> 4e3

4000.0

>>> type (4.)

<class 'float'>

>>> .2e2

20.0

>>> 1.1 + 2. 2 # is represented with
binary floating point error

3.3000000000000003
```

Booleans

The type of data to represent logical or Boolean values in Python is bool, in Pascal and C++ they are defined as boolean and bool, respectively. Boolean data takes the value True (1 logical) or False (0 logical). The Boolean name is used after George Boole, an English mathematician, proposed in the 19th century an algebraic system based on these two logical values and three logical operations: "and logical", "or logical" and negation. Examples:

```
>>> a = 3 > 2

>>> a

True

>>> type(a)

<class 'bool'>

>>> 4 > 5

False
```

Character

The type of character data used in several programming languages is the scalar or indivisible element of the texts used in computer science. The texts are called a character string. For example, the ASCII characters ordered from decimal value 20 to 127 are:

```
! " # $ % & ' ( ) * +, -. / 0 1 2 3 4 5 6
7 8 9:; < = > ? @ A B
```

```
C D E F G H I J K L M N O P Q R S T U
V W X Y Z [ \] ^ _ ` a b c d
e f g h i j k l m n o p q r s t u v w x y z
{|} ~
```

The order in which they are represented serves to evaluate which is greater than another, according to the numerical value in which they appear in the ASCII code. For example, 'b' is greater than 'a'.

The character type is not defined in Python. Simple characters are defined just like a text with a single letter, that is, as a string of characters (string).

```
>>> type('a')
<class 'str'>
```

It can be seen that the character 'a' in Python is of type string (str), although in other languages such as Pascal it would be of type character (char).

Composite or structured data

Composite or structured data includes data with elements of values of the same type or of different types, which are represented unified to be saved or processed.

Characterized string data: string

The string data type is the basic structure for handling text, which includes alphanumeric characters and other characters of the ASCII or UTF-8 encoding. Strings in Python are defined in single ('') or double ("") quotes. They can also be defined in triple quotes ("" ") when multiple lines are thrown. For example,

```
>>> 'Hi'

'Hi'

>>> b = "Wooden house"

>>> type(b)

<class 'str'>

>>> type (15)

<class 'int'>

>>> type ('15')

<class 'str'>
```

The texts 'Hi' or "Wooden house" are of type string in general in all languages. The value 15 is an integer type number (int), however, the value '15' is a string (str). If quotes (") or single quotes (') are included within a string, they may give erroneous results when these characters are used to delimit the string. You can use the character that has not been used as a delimiter within the text:

```
>>> 'She said "Cute"'

'She said "Cute"'

>>> "He doesn't know"

"He doesn't know"
```

However, in these cases you can also use the backslash character (\) that serves as an escape to add quotes or other actions within the string:

```
>>> print ('He doesn\'t know I
\"will come\"')

He doesn't know I "will come"
```

The backslash character (called escape character) followed by n (\ n) indicates jump to a new line. Multiple lines can be included in a string using triple quotes "" "..." "". In this case, line ends are included. Jump to a new line can be seen when they appear on the screen with the internal print function ():

```
>>> print ('We change line \ new
line')
```

```
We change line

New line

>>> "" "

Program:

Author:

Date:" ""

'\ n Program: \ n Author: \ n Date:
\ n'
```

Variables and assignment action

In mathematics, variables are used to represent numerical values. A character or text is used to represent them. In mathematical calculation, a function of the type y = f (x) involves two variables, x, and y.

In programming languages, it is usually required to remember or save the numerical, Boolean or text values to be used once or multiple times in the program. The variables have this task. In languages such as FORTRAN, C / C++ or Pascal, a variable is considered a container or place within the computer's RAM, with an associated name (identifier), where a value of a certain type is stored. By using computer programs, we can stick with this concept. However, in Python, the concept is somewhat different, since the variables are not a place of memory that contains a value but are associated, or refer to, a place of memory that contains that value. The values can be an integer, real, boolean, etc.

Expressions and sentences

Expressions are the mechanism to make calculations and consist of combinations of values and identifiers with operators. They can include variables, data, operators, parentheses and functions that return results.

Every expression has a value that is the result of evaluating it from left to right, considering the precedents. Examples of expressions:

```
>>> 1.5*3/2

2.25

>>> 1.2*x + 3 # The value of x in the
previous example is 10.0

15.0

>>> 3 > (3.1 + 2)/3

True
```

The sentences or instructions are the basic units of the programs (also called in the slang of the programmers, codes) that produces an action, such as assigning a value to a variable, displaying a result, etc. The Python interpreter executes each statement producing the given action.

```
>>> y = x/2 + 3

>>> print(y)

8.0
```

```
>>>
1.5*3/2
2.25
>>> print
(_)
2.25
```

The first sentence in the box on the left calculates the expression x / 2 + 3 and the result assigns it to the variable y. The second statement shows the value of y. But, the expression in the box on the right 1.5 * 3/2, whose calculation is not assigned to any variable, its result is saved associated with a variable called "_".

Operators

The operators are the symbols that represent the calculation actions. In addition to classical mathematical operations, logical and relationship or comparison operators are used in programming. We can classify the operators of 3 types: arithmetic operators, logical or Boolean operators, and relational operators.

Arithmetic operators

Operation	Operator	Expression	Result type
Sum	+	a+b	Integer if a and b integers; real if any is real
Subtraction	-	a-b	Integer if a and b integers; real if any is real
Multiplication	*	a*b	Integer if a and b integers; real if any is real
Division, a ÷ b (integer)	/	a/b	Always real
Division, integer	//	a//b	Returns the whole part of the quotient a ÷ b
Module, rest	%	a%b	Returns the rest of the division a ÷ b
Exponentiation, ab	**	a**b	Integer if a and b integers; real if any is real

Examples:

```
>>> 14/4         # Integer Division
3.5
>>> 14 // 4         # Division, returns whole part of dividing 14 by 4
3
>>> 14% 4       # Module, returns the rest of dividing 14 by 4
2
```

Arithmetic operators that operate on a single operand are called unary: sign change operator - and identity + operator. For example, -4, +4, --4 equals 4.

The Importance of Data Visualization

Before we can finish off our own data analysis, we need to take some time to learn about data visualization and how we are able to utilize this for some of our needs. These visuals are amazing because they can take all of the data that we have collected and sorted through and analyzed from before and puts it into a format that we can read and understand. Visuals and graphs are a whole lot easier to look through and gain the main meaning from than reading through reports and spreadsheets, which is why these data visuals are going to be such an important part of this process. With this in mind, we are going to dive in and take a look at the data visualizations and what we are able to do with them.

The Background of Data Visualization

To start with, we need to understand that data visualization is just going to be the presentation of data in a graphical or a pictorial format. It is going to enable some decision-makers to look through the analytics that we did with all of our data, but it is done in a visual manner. This will help everyone involved grasp difficult concepts or identify some new patterns that are important. Moreover, we even have the chance to work with visualizations that are a bit more interactive, which helps us to take this concept a bit further. This helps us to use a lot of our modern technology in order to drill down into the charts and graphs to find more details and can help us to change the data we see interactively, and process it to meet our needs.

With that information in mind, it is time for us to look a bit at some of the histories that are possible with data visuals. The concept of using pictures and graphs to look through data and understand it a bit more has been around for centuries. For example, how many times did travelers and even those who have gone to war worked with maps to help them see what is going on and to figure out what they did next?

Visuals can help us to figure out what kind of business we are looking at, can help us to separate out things in a group, and can even help with making maps and working with things like temperatures and geographical features that we need as well. This is a big reason why we would want to work with these to help with our data visualization.

The technology that comes in our modern world has really lit a big fire under data visualization and how it works for our needs. Computers have made it possible to go through and process a huge amount of data, and we are able to do it at incredibly high speeds as well. Moreover, because of this, we can see that data visualizations is a big blend of art and science that is already having a large impact over the corporate landscape over the next few years.

There are a lot of ways that we are able to work with these data visuals, and taking the time to learn how to use them, and to learn all of the different ways that you can work with these to help you understand what data you are taking in and what it means for you, can make all of the difference in how well you can use your own data.

Why is Data Visualization so Important?

Now that we have had a chance to talk about data visualizations a bit, it is important to understand why this is something that is so important. Why can't we just go through the analysis and then understand the information that is there? There are many reasons why you should work with the data analysis and why it is such an important part of the process that you should focus on.

Data visualization is going to be one of the quick and easy methods that help to convey all of these concepts in an easy to understand manner.

Think about how much you are able to fit into one of these visuals. Even language barriers are not such a big deal because we know what is found in the data just by looking at the image. And we can use one image to tell us a lot about the process and the data that we are working with, something that could take up pages of complicated jargon to do when we work with it on a spreadsheet or another document. This is all possible and easy to work with when we work on extensions to the Python language, such as the Matplotlib library that we talked about before.

In addition to some of the topics that we learned above, there are a few other ways that we are able to work with data visualization. Some of these are going to include:

The data visuals are going to help us to figure out which areas in our business are more likely toned some improvement and some of our attention.

These data visuals are going to help us to clarify which factors are more likely to influence the behavior of other customers.

These data visuals are going to make it easier to understand which products should be placed in different locations.

When they are used in the proper manner, these data visuals are going to be able to help a company predict their volume of sales so that they can do other things inside of the business to reduce waste and make more money.

Moreover, these are just a few of the things that the data visuals are going to be able to do for us. Moreover, with all of the different options that we can choose when it comes to working with data visuals, from pie charts, bar graphs, and so much more. This helps us to handle any and all of the data that we want in a safe and secure manner, while really seeing what information is hidden inside of it.

How Can We Use Data Visualization?

The next thing that we need to look at here is how these visuals are being used in the first place. No matter how big the industry is, all businesses are working with data visualization to help them make more sense of their data overall. In addition, there are varieties of methods that can be used to help with this one. Some of the ways that companies are working with data visualizations include:

It can help them to comprehend the information they are working with much better. By using graphs for the information of the business, it is easier for these companies to see a large amount of data in a manner that is more cohesive and clear. Moreover, they can then draw better conclusions from that information. Moreover, because it is always a lot easier for the brain to analyze information in a format that is graphic, rather than looking through spreadsheets and other methods, businesses are able to address problems and even answer questions in a more timely manner.

How to Lay the Groundwork

Before you take some time to implement some new technology, there are a number of steps that all businesses need to be able to take. Not only do you need to have a nice solid grasp on the data at hand, but we also need to be able to understand our goals, needs, and the audience we are working with. Preparing your organization for the technology that has to come with these data visuals is going to require that we can do the following first:

We need to have a good understanding of the data that we want to visualize. This includes the size and how unique the values in the charts are going to be to one another.

We need to be able to determine what we would like to visualize and what information we are hoping to communicate when we pick out a chart or a graph to use.

We need to have a good understanding of our audience and then understand how this audience is going to process information in a visual manner.

We need to use some visuals that can convey the information in the best and the simplest form that we can so that our audience is able to understand what is going on.

Once you have been able to meet some of these needs about the data you are working with and the audience who you plan to consume your products, then it is time for us to get prepared for data we would like to work with. Big data is going to bring in new challenges to the work of visualization because we are able to see some of the larger volumes and the varieties that are there. Even some of the changes in the velocities are going to be important when we work here so we cannot forget all about this. In addition, the data that we will use can be generated in a much faster than we can analyze it and manage it in most cases.

We can then use this to help pinpoint some emerging trends that will show up in the data. Working on these kinds of visuals is a good idea because it will help us to find some of the trends that are in the market, and some of the business trends that are important. When we can find these, and we use them in the right way, it helps us to get the most out of our competition. Moreover, of course, this is a good way to affect your bottom line as well. It is easier to spot some of the outliers that would affect the quality of the product or some of the customer churn, and then you can address these issues before they turn into a bigger problem.

Identify some of the patterns and relationships that will show up. Even extensive amounts of data that may seem complicated to go through can make more sense when you present it in a graphical format. Moreover, you will find that businesses using this can find all of the parameters that are there and how much they will correlate with one another. You will find that a few of these are going to be obvious, and you may not need this data analysis to get it to work, but others are harder to find. The graphs and charts that you want to use can help the company focus on the best areas, the ones that are the most likely to influence their goals the most.

Finally, these visuals are going to be good at communicating the story to others. Once the business has been able to go through and uncover some new insights from these analytics, the next part of the process will include what we need in order to talk about these insights and show what they are to others. It is possible to work with charts and even some graphs and any of the some of the other representations that are impactful and fun to look at because it can engage and can help to get the message across as quickly as possible.

As we can see here, there are a lot of benefits to working with these visuals, and being able to add them to your data analysis is going to make a big difference overall. Companies in all industries are able to go through and work with some of the visuals to help them understand the data that they are analyzing in a manner that is easier than anything else is. You cannot go wrong adding in some of these visuals to your work and ensuring that you can fully understand what is going on in your data.

Indexing and selecting arrays

Generating Arrays

There are different ways of creating arrays. The examples above illustrate the simplest, by creating a sequence or a list in the form of an argument with the array() function. Below is an example:

```
>>> x = np.array([[5, 7, 9],[6, 8, 10]])

>>> x

array([[5, 7, 9],

[6, 8, 10]])
```

Other than the lists created, you can also create one or more tuples in the same manner as shown below using the array() function:

```
>>> x = np.array(((5, 7, 9),(6, 8, 10)))

>>> x

array([[5, 7, 9],

[6, 8, 10]])
```

Alternatively, you can also use the same procedure to create more than one tuple as shown below:

```
>>> x = np.array([(1, 4, 9), [2, 4, 6], (3, 6, 9)])

>>> x
```

array([[1, 4, 9],

[2, 4, 6],

[3, 6, 9]])

As you work with ndarrays, you will come across different types of data. Generally, you will be dealing with numerical values a lot, especially float and integer values. However, the NumPy library is built to support more than those two. The following are other data types that you will use in NumPy:

- bool_
- int_
- intc, intp, int8, int16
- uint8, uint16, uint32, uint64
- float_, float16, float32, float64
- complex64, complex128

Each of the NumPy numerical types mentioned above has a unique function used to call its value as shown below:

Input

float64(52)

Output

52.0

Input

int8(52.0)

Output

52

Input

bool(52)

Output

True

Input

bool(0)

Output

False

Input

bool(52.0)

Output

True

Input

float(True)

Output

1.0

Input

float(False)

Output

0.0

Some of the functions might need a data type to complete the argument as shown below:

Input:

arrange (6, dtype=uint16)

Output:

array ([0, 1, 2, 3, 4, 5], dtype=uint16)

Before you create a multidimensional array, you must know how to create a vector as shown below:

a = arange(4)

a.dtype

Output

dtype('int64')

a

Output

array([0, 1, 2, 3])

a.shape

Output

(4,)

The vector outlined above has only four components. The value of the components is between 0 and 3.

To create a multidimensional array, you must know the shape of the array as shown below:

```
x = array([arange(2), arange(2)])

x
```

Output

```
array([[0, 1],

[0, 1]])
```

To determine the shape of the array, use the following function:

```
x.shape
```

Output

```
(2, 2)
```

The arrange() function has been used to build a 2 x 2 array.

You will come across situations where you need to choose only one aspect of an array and ignore the rest. Before you begin, create a 2 x 2 matrix as shown below:

```
a = array([[10,20],[30,40]])

a
```

Output

```
array([[10, 20],

[30, 40]])
```

From the array above, we are going to select an item. Keep in mind that the index numbers in NumPy always start from 0.

Input: a (0, 0)

Output:

10

Input: a (0, 10)

Output

20

Input: a (10, 0)

Output

30

Input: a (10, 10)

Output

40

From the example above, you can see how easy it is to select specific elements from an array. Given an array a, as above, we have the notation a(x, y) where x and y represent the indices of each object within the array, a.

From time to time you might come across character codes. It is important to know the data types associated with them as follows:

Character codeData type

bbool

ddouble precision float

Dcomplex

fsingle precision float

iinteger

Sstring

uunsigned integer

Uunicode

Vvoid

For example, a single precision floats array can be identified as shown below:

Input:

arrange (5, dtype='f')

Output:

array ([0, 1, 2, 3, 4], dtype=f;pat32)

Slicing and Indexing

You learned about slicing standard Python lists in the other books in this series. The same knowledge applies when slicing one-dimensional NumPy arrays. You will also learn how to flatten arrays. Flattening arrays simply means converting a multidimensional array into a one-dimensional array.

The ravel() function can manipulate the shape of an array as follows:

Input

b

Output

array([[[0, 1, 2, 3],

[4, 5, 6, 7]]])

Input

b.ravel ()

Output

array([0, 1, 2, 3, 4, 5, 6, 7])

The flatten() function performs the same task as ravel(). However, the difference is that in the flatten function, the array is allocated new memory.

It is possible to set the shape of a tuple without using the reshape() function. This is done as follows:

Input

b.shape = (3,4)

Input

b

Output

array

([[0, 1, 2, 3],

[4, 5, 6, 7],

[8, 9, 10, 11])

Transposition is a common procedure in linear algebra where you convert the rows into columns and columns into rows. Using the example above, we will have the following output:

Input

b.transpose = ()

Output:

array

([[0, 4, 8],

[1, 5, 9],

[2, 6, 10],

[3, 7, 11])

It is possible to stack an array by the depth, vertical alignment, or horizontal alignment. For this purpose, you will use the following functions:

- hstack()
- dstack()
- vstack()

For a horizontal stack, the ndarray tuple is as shown below:

Input:

hstack((a, b))

For a vertical stack, the ndarray tuple is as shown below:

Input:

vstack((a, b))

For a depth stack, the ndarray tuple is as shown below:

Input:

dstack((a, b))

Common Debugging Tools

When you are working on some of the codes you would like to write in Python, there are going to be some times when things go wrong. The code may not work the way you would like, and little issues and bugs can become a problem for you to handle. It is important to know more about which tools you can use to not only prevent these bugs along the way, but to make sure you can fix them if one does show up in the coding you try to do with Python.

The neat thing about working with Python is it comes with a lot of different debugging tools. This is going to make it easier to check up on the code you are doing and to ensure you can get it to work the way you would like. There are tools that allow you to work from the command line, as well as from the IDE, and even some analysis tools that are going to come in and help you prevent some of these bugs in the first place.

Debugging Your IDE

The IDE, or Integrated Development Environment, is a great place to start when it is time to start on your big project in Python. This is also an important place where we are going to work on the debugging process because it has direct interaction with some of the coding you do in Python.

Now, you will quickly notice that the debugging tools you can use for your IDE will vary depending on what kind of IDE you would like to use. The good news is they all are going to have the same kind of features to get the work done, including the steps of running the code, setting the breakpoints, and examining the variable.

There are a lot of options when it is time to work with the IDE you would like to use. Whether you choose to go with one that comes with Python to keep things easier and to just download everything at once or you plan to use the specialized version you can find, you will see that it is easier to find a debugging tool for your version just by doing a simple search. Many of them are going to come with a similar kind of workflow so you're able to pick out the one that is the best for your needs.

Options for Debugging

There are a lot of different debugging tools we can use in order to get started with this process in our program. Learning which ones can handle some of the work we want to do and can ensure our programs work in a smooth manner as we want is going to be important. Some of the different options you can choose when it is time to work on the debugging process in Python include:

Pdb: This works on all of the major operating systems. This is going to be seen as the standard library debugger. The neat thing is that it comes with the installations of Python you already have.

Pudb: This one is going to work with Mac OS X and Unix. This is a visual console-based and even a full-screen debugger that has been designed as a more comfortable replacement that we can use when compared to the option above.

HAP Python Remote Debugger: This is a debugger that works well with the Windows system. It is going to provide us with the ability to debug our system from a remote location.

Windpdb and Rpdb2: This one is going to work on Windows, Linux, and Unix: We will see this one as a more advanced Python debugger, with support for some of the smarter breakpoints, embedded debugging, encrypted communication, changes to the namespaces, and multiple threads. It is also faster than some of the other options.

Rpdb: This one will work with Unix, Mac OS X, and Windows: This is the predecessor to the option we just talked about above and it is going to improve some of the usability we see with pdbs and adds in some of the support needed to handle the remote debugging. It is also going to come with the ability to debug embedded scripts, post mortem of unhandled exceptions, and the ability to debug more than one thread at a time

JpyDbg: This one is going to work with Windows, VMS, Unix, OS/2, and Mac OS X. It is going to be both a JPYTHON and CPYTHON debugging framework that has been changed up so it works as well inside of Jedit as a standard Jedit plugin.

DDD: This one will work with the Unix operating system. It is going to be a graphical command-line debugger that will help us to handle some of the debugging we would like to get done in our code.

Pyclewn: This works well with Unix and Windows: This one is going to allow the programmer to use Vim as their front end to get the work done that they would like.

Pdb++: This one is going to work with Mac OS X, Windows, and Unix. This is going to be a kind of extension from the pdb module we saw with our standard library and it is meant to be compatible with the predecessor as much as possible. The good news is it is still going to introduce a number of new features to make the experience of debugging as easy aspossible.

Python-pydebug: And finally, we are going to look at this debugger that works well with Unix, Mac OS X, and Windows. This is a set of debugging decorators that will respect the settings for Django within our coding. It will allow a user the ability to turn PDB into a function, inspect an object, work with a line profiler, and even to disassemble the function if needed.

Preventing the Bugs

Of course, one of the best things you can do for your own coding and your own program is to make sure none of those bugs get into the program in the first place. In the beginning, this is going to be hard and you may worry that your code is never going to work because you get a bug in it. But the more you practice and learn about these debugging tools, the easier it is going to be to avoid some of these bugs and to make sure the coding is going to work the way you would like.

Learning how to prevent some of these bugs, or at least keep them down to a minimum when you are first starting with your coding journey, can be important. So far, we have spent our time talking about some of the reactive tools out there for finding and fixing the bugs that do show up. But what if we were able to prevent these bugs from showing up in the first place?

This is where a number of analysis tools are going to come into play for us. Using these tools will give us a handle on where the code is going. One thing to keep in mind with this though is that your code may not always go to a good place like you want it to. Some of the tools you can use in order to pre-debug your code include:

Pylint: This is known as a linter because it can look over the code you have and then make some suggestions on the things you can improve on within that code.

Pycodestyle: This is a good tool to use because it will make some recommendations for you and about how you should format the code you want to work with. The idea with this one is that if your code can follow some of the standard conventions, then it is easier to have other Python programmers take a look at it and gain a better understanding in no time.

Flake8: This is going to be one of those tools you will want to use all of the time. It is going to come with both of the two features we talked about in one, along with a few other features as well. This makes it easier to have all of the tools you need to check the code and make sure it is working well.

Neural Network and What to Use for?

Regular deep neural networks commonly receive a single vector as an input and then transform it through a series of multiple hidden layers. Every hidden layer in regular deep neural networks, in fact, is made up of a collection of neurons in which every neuron is fully connected to all contained neurons from the previous layers. In addition, all neurons contained in a deep neural network are completely independent as they do not share any relations or connections.

The last fully-connected layer in regular deep neural networks is called the output layer and in every classification setting, this output layer represents the overall class score.

Due to these properties, regular deep neural nets are not capable of scaling to full images. For instance, in CIFAR-10, all images are sized as 32x32x3. This means that all CIFAR-10 images gave 3 color channels and that they are 32 wide and 32 inches high. This means that a single fully-connected neural network in a first regular neural net would have 32x32x3 or 3071 weights. This is an amount that is not manageable as those fully-connected structures are not capable of scaling to larger images.

In addition, you would want to have more similar neurons to quickly add-up more parameters. However, in this case of computer vision and other similar problems, using fully-connected neurons is wasteful as your parameters would lead to over-fitting of your model very quickly. Therefore, convolutional neural networks take advantage of the fact that their inputs consist of images for solving these kinds of deep learning problems.

Due to their structure, convolutional neural networks constrain the architecture of images in a much more sensible way. Unlike a regular deep neural network, the layers contained in the convolutional neural network are comprised of neurons that are arranged in three dimensions including depth, height, and width. For instance, the CIFAR-10 input images are part of the input volume of all layers contained in a deep neural network and the volume comes with the dimensions of 32x32x3.

The neurons in these kinds of layers can be connected to only a small area of the layer before it, instead of all the layers being fully-connected like in regular deep neural networks. In addition, the output of the final layers for CIFAR-10 would come with dimensions of 1x1x10 as the end of convolutional neural networks architecture would have reduced the full image into a vector of class score arranging it just along the depth dimension.

To summarize, unlike the regular-three-layer deep neural networks, a ConvNet composes all its neurons in just three dimensions. In addition, each layer contained in convolutional neural network transforms the 3D input volume into a 3D output volume containing various neuron activations.

A convolutional neural network contains layers that all have a simple API resulting in 3D output volume that comes with a differentiable function that may or may not contain neural network parameters.

How Convolutional Neural Networks Work?

A convolutional neural network structure of ConvNet is normally used for various deep learning problems. As already mentioned, convolutional neural networks are used for object recognition, object segmentation, detection and computer vision due to their structure. Convolutional neural networks, in fact, learn directly from image data, so there is no need to perform manual feature extraction which is commonly required in regular deep neural networks.

The use of convolutional neural networks has become popular due to three main factors. The first of them is the structure of CNNs, which eliminates the need for performing manual data extraction as all data features are learned directly by the convolutional neural networks. The second reason for the increasing popularity of convolutional neural networks is that they produce amazing, state-of-art object recognition results. The third reason is that convolutional neural networks can be easily retained for many new object recognition tasks to help build other deep neural networks.

A CNN can contain hundreds of layers, which each learn automatically to detect many different features of an image data. In addition, filters are commonly applied to every training image at different resolutions, so the output of every convolved image is used as the input to the following convolutional layer.

Convolutional Neural Networks Applications

Convolutional neural networks are one of the main categories of deep neural networks which have proven to be very effective in numerous computer science areas like object recognition, object classification, and computer vision. ConvNets have been used for many years for distinguishing faces apart, identifying objects, powering vision in self-driving cars, and robots.

A ConvNet can easily recognize countless image scenes as well as suggest relevant captions. ConvNets are also able to identify everyday objects, animals or humans, as well. Lately, convolutional neural networks have also been used effectively in natural language processing problems like sentence classification.

Therefore, convolutional neural networks are one of the most important tools when it comes to machine learning and deep learning tasks. LeEnt was the very first convolutional neural network introduced that helped significantly propel the overall field of deep learning. This very first convolutional neural network was proposed by Yann LeCun back in 1988. It was primarily used for character recognition problems such as reading digits and codes.

Convolutional neural networks that are regularly used today for innumerable computer science tasks are very similar to this first convolutional neural network proposed back in 1988.

Just like today's convolutional neural networks, LeNet was used for many character recognition tasks. Just like in LeNet, the standard convolutional neural networks we use today come with four main operations including convolution, ReLU non-linearity activation functions, sub-sampling or pooling and classification of their fully-connected layers.

Stride and Padding

Secondly, after specifying the depth, you also must specify the stride that you slide over the filter. When you have a stride that is one, you must move one pixel at a time. When you have a stride that is two, you can move two pixels at a time, but this produces smaller volumes of output spatially. By default, stride value is one. However, you can have bigger strides in the case when you want to come across less overlap between your receptive fields, but, as already mentioned, this will result in having smaller feature maps as you are skipping over image locations.

In the case when you use bigger strides, but you want to maintain the same dimensionality, you must use padding that surrounds your input with zeros. You can either pad with the values on the edge or with zeros. Once you get the dimensionality of your feature map that matches your input, you can move onto adding pooling layers that padding is commonly used in convolutional neural networks when you want to preserve the size of your feature maps.

If you do not use padding, your feature maps will shrink at every layer. Adding zero-padding is times very convenient when you want to pad your input volume just with zeros all around the border.

This is called as zero-padding which is a hyperparameter. By using zero-padding, you can control the size of your output volumes.

You can easily compute the spatial size of your output volume as a simple function of your input volume size, the convolution layers receptive field size, the stride you applied and the amount of zero-padding you used in your convolutional neural network border.

Parameter Sharing

You can use a parameter sharing scheme in your convolutional layers to entirely control the number of used parameters. If you denoted a single two-dimensional slice of depth as your depth slice, you can constrain the neurons contained in every depth slice to use the same bias and weights. Using parameter sharing techniques, you will get a unique collection of weights, one of every depth slice, and you will get a unique collection of weights. Therefore, you can significantly reduce the number of parameters contained in the first layer of your ConvNet. Doing this step, all neurons in every depth slice of your ConvNet will use the same parameters.

In other words, during backpropagation, every neuron contained in the volume will automatically compute the gradient for all its weights.

However, these computed gradients will add up over every depth slice, so you get to update just a single collection of weights per depth slice.that all neurons contained in one depth slice will use the exact same weight vector. Therefore, when you forward pass of the convolutional layers in every depth slice, it is computed as a convolution of all neurons' weights alongside the input volume. This is the reason why we refer to the collection of weights we get as a kernel or a filter, which is convolved with your input.

However, there are a few cases in which this parameter sharing assumption, in fact, does not make any sense. This is commonly the case with many input images to a convolutional layer that come with certain centered structure, where you must learn different features depending on your image location.

For instance, when you have an input of several faces which have been centered in your image, you probably expect to get different hair-specific or eye-specific features that could be easily learned at many spatial locations. When this is the case, it is very common to just relax this parameter sharing scheme and simply use a locally-connected layer.

Matrix Multiplication

The convolution operation commonly performs those dot products between the local regions of the input and between the filters. In these cases, a common implementation technique of the convolutional layers is to take full advantage of this fact and to formulate the specific forward pass of the main convolutional layer representing it as one large matrix multiply.

Implementation of matrix multiplication is when the local areas of an input image are completely stretched out into different columns during an operation known as im2col. For instance, if you have an input of size 227x227x3 and you convolve it with a filter of size 11x11x3 at a stride of 4, you must take blocks of pixels in size 11x11x3 in the input and stretch every block into a column vector of size 363.

However, when you iterate this process in your input stride of 4, you get fifty-five locations along both weight and height that lead to an output matrix of x col in which every column contained in fact is a maximally stretched out receptive fields and where you have 3025 fields in total.

Conclusion

This is the last part of the book. Thank you for making it through to the end of this book, let's hope it was informative and able to provide you with all of the tools you need to achieve your goals whatever they may be.

The next step is to start learning how you are able to implement the basics of data science and Python into your own business as well. These are big buzzwords that have been flying around the world of business, no matter what industry the business is in, and many companies are ready to jump right in and see what this data science can do for them. But actually, taking some of the steps that are needed and learning how to work with the data life cycle and all of the different processes that we need with this can make a difference, and taking that first step can be hard. This guidebook has taken the time to look at all of these different parts to explore how a business can get started with data science for their own needs.

There are a lot of different parts that come with the data science life cycle, and while it may seem like more fun to just create the model and be done with it, all of these steps are going to be very important to the results that we are looking to get. We have to work through the collection of raw data, cleaning off and organizing the data that we have, learning what insights are there, figuring out the best model to work with and training and testing it, and then completing the analysis as well. We will take some time to discuss all of these parts and more as we worked through this guidebook and figure out the best way to make these works for us as well.

The data science process is going to provide you with a ton of benefits overall, and you are going to enjoy how it is going to be in order to use this information to learn more about your customers, about your competition and more, so you can increase your bottom line and see some results with your business. It may take some time, and often it may take some programming knowledge and more to get it done. But you will find that with the help of the Python coding language, and some of the machine learning that we have learned in this guidebook, you will be able to make this work for your needs.

Working with data science is something that all businesses are able to use to help them get ahead and really see some results in the process. But it is a process that takes time and is not always as easy to complete as we might hope. With the help of this guidebook, and some of the tools that we have learned inside, get ready to use Python data science for your needs. I hope this book helped you with whatever you were looking for.

www.ingramcontent.com/pod-product-compliance
Lightning Source LLC
LaVergne TN
LVHW082035050326
832904LV00005B/192